Go Dartmouth!

Stuart Anderson (signature)

Corporate Cowboy

How Maverick Entrepreneur
Stuart Anderson built
Black Angus, the
Number 1 Restaurant Chain
of the 1980s

By Stuart Anderson

Published and Printed in the USA

Corporate Cowboy
How Maverick Entrepreneur Stuart Anderson built Black Angus,
the Number 1 Chain of the 1980s
Copyright @ 2014 by Stuart Anderson

Cataloging-in-Publication Data is on file with the Library of Congress

ISBN: 9780692200636
Non-Fiction Restaurant Memoirs

The opinions and information provided are based on
my personal experience as the founder of Black Angus and are not
necessarily those of current owners of the restaurant chain, of which
I am no longer affiliated - nor do I own any portion or profit from any
part of that business.

Unless noted, all photos are from my personal collection
of which I own all rights. The newspaper clippings are copies of
articles either written about me or that I and my company were
mentioned and we have cited sources accordingly.

Cover and Book Design: Laura Dobbins
ferless74@yahoo.com

Editors:
Lucinda Sue Crosby,luckycinda@yahoo.com
& Kathryn Jordan

Helen Anderson also contributed countless hours to this project.

Printed and Published in the USA

First Edition: 2014

Dedication

I would like to dedicate this book to all the people who helped me achieve my success because it is certainly not anything I could have done on my own. I learned a lot from you and hopefully you learned something from me. Unfortunately, there are way too many folks to name but you know who you are.

So, for my wife Helen, who was literally my right hand, thanks from the bottom of my heart.

I would also like to thank Lucinda and Laura of LuckyCinda for getting this book published. I am a victim of their charms.

TABLE OF CONTENTS

Preface

....

Welcome to my world; it's a pistol!

Those that know about such things tell me this is a "memoir," meaning it's basically my life and times but more how I remember what happened than just the facts, ma'am. I have included my thoughts and feelings along with some hard-learned lessons that served me well over the years.

And although I've been a rancher, this is not a book about beef – it's about me and my relationship with the most successful chain of the 1980s (just before I retired): Stuart Anderson's Black Angus/Cattle Company Restaurants.

As a kind of bonus, you'll also find some delicious recipes covering Black Angus signature favorites, my personal favorites and dishes suitable for diabetics, as I have lived with that condition for almost 40 years.

There are three things you oughta know from the get-go:

1. This is NOT a commercial. I no longer own any restaurants or one head of cattle or one acre of ranch land.

2. I'm a plain-speaking guy and I write like I talk.

3. I firmly believe that one moment can actually change a life.

The first Stuart Anderson's Black Angus opened in 1964, 50 years ago as I write this. I started my first book, *HERE'S THE BEEF!* 25 years ago. I've emphasized some of the chapters from that previous book because the restaurant portion is necessarily part of this story.

But as I approached my 90th birthday, as the memories and attending emotions began flooding back into my mind, I realized how much more there was to tell. Almost without realizing it, I started strolling, once again, down that long road back and became reacquainted with the drive and focus that used to be second nature.

I am so grateful to all the people who worked with me to build the number one chain. This includes the many great executives, managers and on down the line to the chefs, bookkeepers, servers, kitchen help, bussers, etc.

There were over 10,000 folks who helped me achieve this success.

To the reader, I'd like to know your name but my family already has to wear I.D. tags when we get together, so forget it. I do hope you'll find the book fun and interesting and I appreciate your time and attention.

Stuart Anderson

Corporate Cowboy

Introduction

As I sat there on my tractor watching the sun set over and into the Pacific Ocean, there came a sight that remains frozen in my memory to this day. Heading right at me, straight through the bean field, was a huge, lumbering monster making a horrendous racket and spitting fire and clouds of mist. Although it wasn't quite dark, I could make out the eye of this thing, which was bright with a hood over it like a bonnet. As it sped toward me, hell bent for leather, the whole field started to shake and while I hate to admit it, I got more than somewhat spooked. I probably looked like a deer caught in the headlights of a car.

What had I gotten into?

I was just a kid on the first day of my new job. It was mid-season and I was trying to earn some money for my freshman year at the University of Southern California. My temporary position was on the Janss Corporation's company ranch near Ventura, where I harvested lima beans. I had never farmed before but I loved it – but not because of those beans! (I've never put them on a menu nor do I eat them with any great glee.)

I didn't mind the long hours … but no one had prepared me for this terrifying apparition.

Running alongside the field where I worked was a railroad track I hadn't noticed before. It suddenly dawned on me that my monster was a steam-powered engine pulling the famous Daylight Train on its route from San Francisco to L.A. The train had just left the city of Ventura and was chugging up a slight incline on the way to its next stop in the Simi Valley. I swear it came within a couple of yards of me and the force of its passing about blew me off my seat. The hood on the headlight, I know now, was a seemingly useless precaution taken at the time of the "blackout." It was 1942, you see, and since our country had just declared war, there was a fear of invasion by the Japanese. The Ventura area seemed especially vulnerable following the surprising previous appearance of a Japanese submarine just up the coast.

In the deepening shadow of evening, I noticed that the train's window shades had not yet been drawn, as required by blackout regulations. I stared with fascination into those windows, captivated by the range of activities passing me by in what seemed like slow motion. As the dining car and then the observation car clickety-clacked past, I had a revelation. The well-dressed passengers were living in the joy of the moment, and they looked happy and glamorous and beautiful.

I'm sure this world of high excitement was made even more appealing by the envy of one lonely kid.

As the cars disappeared, the red taillight bobbing as if waving good-bye, I was left wondering all kinds of things. And it was at that very moment I realized I couldn't get THERE … to the glamorous life of the people in those cars, from HERE … ranching for minimum wage. It hit me that ranching, as good as it is working with animals and being in the great outdoors, was hard work for low pay and would never provide a financially sound route to a ride on that beautiful train.

It's also because of that experience that I don't think I was much of a rancher before I was a restaurateur.

But before we leap ahead of ourselves, we must return to the location of the train incident and my restaurant endeavors. In between, there came a dance with that devil, Adolf Hitler, who managed to alter the lives of people in

Coast Daylight was a passenger train originally run by the Southern Pacific Railroad (SP) between the cities of Los Angeles and San Francisco, California, via SP's Coast Line.

many nations and take a few years out of my personal schedule in the bargain.

Early on, I have included stories about my years driving a tank in General George Patton's Army. Why? Because they had a strong effect on my life's outlook. Let me tell you, it is tough living inside a tank with four other men who often had to go weeks without a shower. Your social life is so monotonous, you can't even use the word "social." It consisted of chatting with the same guys for months on end about the same tired subjects.

What saved me was that I loved to read and always had a good book to bury myself in. Every time we sat and waited for orders, I would read. If that irritated my buddies because I didn't contribute to the conversation, so be it. It was a great escape.

The war stories as I relate them here are brief but the impression they left behind deepened my desire for that glamorous lifestyle I had witnessed on the train. I started to think about entertainment, show business or anything that was the absolute opposite of where I was at that time. I hope you enjoy my war stories but if you want to pass them by, it won't hurt my feelings. I'll never know!

Incidentally, Adolph was a vegetarian.

Chapter 1

Life is a Marathon and You're in It!

I tried to enlist in the Army Air Force after Pearl Harbor but they said no chance, poor depth perception. When I finished my first year at USC, the draft caught up to me anyway and after completing tank school in Georgia, our battalion was sent to Camp Shanks in New York ...

Eventually the day arrived for boarding the troop carrier bound for Europe and as usual, the Army did everything by the book – alphabetically, with the A's loading first.

I headed one deck down, then another, and still another, down, down, down until I was at the very bottom of the ship. Four bunks were stacked alongside the bulkhead, and lucky me! I was assigned the one on the bottom.

This set-up would make anyone nervous.

For the first time in my life, I realized I had more than a

touch of claustrophobia. Even worse, we were going to cross the Atlantic, which I pictured full of German U-boats, one of which would sink us. A feeling came over me that I'd never make it out of that ship.

My anxiety started to build but panic or no, I had to stay macho. I had to do something or I was dead! But what?

That night, I didn't sleep a wink. The next morning, in the "I swear it's true" category, the ship got stuck leaving the harbor, bringing us to a standstill. Then another troop carrier was brought alongside; they were going to transfer us! We started re-loading, this time in reverse order so the Z's ended up at the bottom. The new ship was a little smaller, and when it came to the A's, the powers that be – I could kiss `em even now – put me and a few others outside on the deck. As I lay there on my little cot looking at the stars, I felt the Bluebird of Happiness watching over me.

There has never been, nor will be again, a luxury cruise ship with such accommodations – and water, water, everywhere.

I was a driver in the Eleventh Tank Battalion, Tenth Armored Division of George Patton's Third Army. The first law of driving a thirty-ton Sherman tank is to make a smooth turn. You steer with levers and go left or right by holding back or stopping one track while the opposite side spins around in a kind of herky-jerky pirouette. Normally, no problem.

However, when we liberated Paris, the population came out in force. Everyone waved white hankies as if surrendering with joy, and in their enthusiasm to greet us, they narrowed the road considerably. Making a turn in that happy mass of humanity was spooky. And while I dreaded running over someone's toes, I don't believe I ever did.

After we camped that night, an acquaintance, who shall remain nameless, and I went into Paris and had a fabulous time. Since we were slightly AWOL, it didn't do my Army career any good.

Day after day, the closer we got to Germany, I clearly remember how the joy of the people in "Mudville" (as we called the series of similar, rain-soaked towns) seemed more and more pronounced. Then a warning order came down from Patton's headquarters not to take anything into our vehicles given to us by people along our route. To this day, I don't know if it was a rumor or a fact, but some poor soldier had supposedly done exactly that and the little "gift" had blown him – and his tank mates – sky high.

In one small town where they seemed especially happy to see us, an attractive lady with a beautiful smile approached the tank. It was a lovely fall day and all was right with the world. As she handed me a loaf of bread in greeting, I just couldn't see myself throwing it back in her face or dropping it like a hot potato. The loaf felt and smelled freshly baked but, believe me, I squeezed it within an inch of its life before taking it inside. And even though I had to share it with my tank mates, it made a memorable dinner. Try as I might, I've never been able to equal the taste sensation of that savory loaf of French bread!

From northern France into southern Germany, I almost always drove with my seat extended up, the hatch open and my head completely out of the vehicle. To drive it any other way was uncomfortable, except when under fire and using our periscope. This was one of those button-down days!

The Germans had a habit of lining up their Tiger or Panther tanks on the side streets of small towns so they could unload their 88 mm guns on our columns as we lumbered down Main Street. If they struck the right spot, those shells could penetrate our armor. When moving at our top speed of twenty plus miles an hour, we were tough to get a bead on so we were much better off facing the enemy guns head on.

It's not hard to understand why those wily Germans would use every trick in the book to make us stop, turning us into a stationary target. The orders from Patton's headquarters made sense: "Keep moving, regardless."

On one particular day, driving through yet another nameless German town, my hatch was closed and I only had the periscope for vision. Suddenly, out in the middle of the street, I saw a temporary corral full of dairy cows that appeared in the periscope to number in the thousands.

I knew what I had to do ... full speed ahead and no stopping.

There are five men in a tank and we were all buttoned in

This is a photo of a typical Sherman tank going through "Mudville"

and couldn't yell. Our excuse for a horn didn't do much. I tell you now, with my love of animals, it was one of the toughest things I ever had to do. I have no idea how many animals were injured or killed but most of them broke out of the corral after hearing the bellows of the maimed. To this day I don't know if there was an 88 cannon aimed at us from down that side street. I liked to believe there was and that I did what I had to do.

I ask all animal rightists of the world: What would you have done?

It was early winter in northern France, so not too cozy. Of course, this traveling tank had no john. And when tents were set up in an encampment, everyone constantly shared bathroom and shower facilities – something I never did get totally comfortable with. As our battalion was moving toward the front line, we no longer parked our tanks in a row or side by side as had been our custom. For defensive reasons we spread out haphazardly all over this pasture.

I remember this next incident well.

A bunch of Army trucks rolled in looking more like a circus convoy than a fighting apparatus. They motored into our pasture and set up tent after tent. What the hell were they doing? Then I noticed that the troops were all black. (Integration at that time was talked about but rarely practiced.) What an odd-looking structure they'd erected. What could it be? Eventually the word got passed around – showers! Oh, happy day!

We got very excited since we'd all gone over two weeks without one. We didn't even mind that the water was lukewarm or that there was a two-minute limit. And those guys weren't fooling. In two minutes, when they shut the water off, you didn't want to be left all soaped up. There was a catwalk above the showers and those black soldiers kept yelling "Move it! Move it! Move it! Get your ass outta there or they'll be calling you sudsy." They could yell all they wanted; I've never had a shower that did my body and spirit more good. Now we could put up with each other a while longer inside that tank.

You will read about the end of the war for me and the irony of it in a later chapter.

But for now, let's get on with the story of *Black Angus*.

Chapter 2

The Sweet Smell of Success

*What a great day! We are opening our 100th restaurant in
Ventura, California, near the site of that bean field.
I think I can see it from here, but I'm not sure. The tractor
is probably rusted out by now ...*

Amazingly, here I am, right back where my dream started years ago. I have anticipated, planned for and worked hard for this goal and everything is right with the world. In my mind's eye and ear, I can still hear the train coming. I can still see those beautiful people. I can still watch the caboose slide by. How could I forget? I can now afford to travel on that train and have done so many times.

From one to one hundred stores was a long, tough, fun filled time with interesting people, lots of luck and some really dumb decisions In hindsight, I would change some things and throughout this book, you'll realize which ones.

To those who say they wouldn't change a thing in their life: Oh, come on!

Stu Who's News

Stuart Anderson's
BLACK / CATTLE
ANGUS COMPANY
RESTAURANTS®

Volume 10 Issue 4   February 1984

Black Angus Day Proclaimed in Ventura

Tim Klein, District Manager; Stuart Anderson; John Sweeney, Manager, receiving plaque at the 100th opening from Ventura Mayor John McWhorter.

Stuart Anderson's Black Angus/Cattle Company Restaurants Are #1

"For the third year in a row, **Restaurants & Institutions** has asked the American public to name its favorite restaurant chains.

And the 1983 winner is ...**Stuart Anderson's Black Angus/Cattle Company**, which satisfied its customers better than any of the leading full-service restaurant chains. The Saga Corporation's chain of mid-priced steak restaurants beat out larger and better-known chains such as..." (continued on page 9)

Our in-house newspaper published by Millie Hodge. No one has ever had more fun than Millie when putting out a newsletter.

The Restaurant Business

Impact on the Economy
According to a Washington, D.C. research
organization: In 2012, the restaurant
industry employed nearly
13 million people, or about 10% of the
total U.S. workforce.

By 2022, the industry is expected to add
1.4 million jobs, with an employment
total of 14.4 million. And there are nearly
a million restaurant locations across
the country!

I just want to give you an idea of how big an industry this is. Hopefully I can answer some of your questions about restaurants. I feel qualified to do so because I was the founder of Stuart Anderson's *Black Angus/Cattle Company* chain which was number one in the nation for several years.

"For the third year in a row,
Restaurants & Institutions, has asked the American
public to name its favorite restaurant chains.
And the 1983 winner is ... **Stuart Anderson's Black
Angus/Cattle Company**, which satisfied its
customers better than any of the leading full-service
restaurant chains ... "

&RESTAURANTS &INSTITUTIONS

■ DINNER HOUSES

Stuart Anderson's Emerges Again as America's Favorite

Stuart Anderson's climbed back into the top spot among all full-service restaurant chains in *R&I*'s Choice in Chains survey for the fourth time in the past five years. Five other dinner house concepts also ranked in the top 10.

In fact, the four most popular restaurant chains are dinner houses. Behind No. 1 Stuart Anderson's are Benihana of Tokyo, which was last year's champion, TGI Friday's and Red Lobster. Bennigan's (No. 8) and Steak & Ale (No. 10) also make the top 10.

Chain Sizzles with the Singles, the Spenders

The things that most attract Americans to restaurants—quality of food, service and cleanliness—are the areas where Stuart Anderson's scored higher than any other dinner house chain in *R&I*'s exclusive Choice in Chains survey.

STUART ANDERSON'S REGAINS TOP SPOT AMONG AMERICA'S FULL-SERVICE RESTAURANTS

After Benihana nudged it from first last year, Stuart Anderson's returns as the most popular full-service restaurant. Fuddruckers, Furr's and Golden Corral broke into the top 10.

Chain	'86	'85
Stuart Anderson's Cattle Co.	1	2
Benihana of Tokyo	2	1
TGI Friday's	3	3
Red Lobster	4	5
Fuddruckers	5	—
Furr's Cafeterias	5*	—
Bennigan's	7	6
Morrison's Cafeterias	8	11
Steak & Ale	8*	4
Golden Corral	10	—
Chi-Chi's	11	9
Bob Evan's	12	19
Shoney's	12*	—
Victoria Station	14	7
Swensen's	15	10
Pizza Hut	16	17
Friendly	15*	14
Western Sizzlin'	18	13
Houlihan's	19	—
Po Folks	20	—
Pizza Inn	21	22
Perkins	22	16
Godfather's Pizza	23	21
Mr. Steak	24	18
Ponderosa	25	25
Sizzler Family Steakhouse	26	15
Bonanza	27	20
Big Boy	28	24
International House of Pancakes	28*	26
Denny's	30	27
Country Kitchen	31	23
Shakey's	32	28
Howard Johnson	33	29

*tie
©1986 *Restaurants & Institutions*, a Cahners publication

In 1983, *Black Angus* was voted number one for casual dining by 98,000 readers of *USA Today*.

For four out of five years in the early to mid-1980s, the company was voted the number one dinner house chain by the readers of *Restaurants & Institutions*, the bible of the industry in those days.

Even though we never made it to the East Coast, we were still voted number one nationally for those years. That was just before I retired in the 1980s.

After Ventura, the chain grew to a total of 122 restaurants in the U.S. and Canada and employed over 10,000 people. Remember, these were all company owned versus franchises.

Note: For those of you who may not know, a franchise is an agreement between a business owner (the franchisor) and another party (the franchisee). This agreement allows the franchisee to use the business name and processes of the franchisor or to market a product or service owned by the franchisor, in exchange for a fee. There are many types of franchises and many ways to structure the agreement.

Through the years, we discovered that each situation was unique and that what we learned from one particular store gave us an advantage in opening those that followed.

Rough and tough but fun and glamorous ... Dream BIG!

Do you dream about working, starting or investing in a restaurant? You're not alone; thousands of Americans share that dream. Yet not everyone has the courage to get started. There are some romantic ideas floating around out there about a career move into this industry, usually held by people who want to share their passion for food with patrons who become like family. For my money, it's the toughest business going. But if you want to own and operate a restaurant, you can. I know because I did it ... and if I can do it, you can do it.

Restaurant chains offering the tastiest experience:

Western-based Stuart Anderson selected as a favorite

Casual dinner houses:

#1
Stuart Anderson
won
high marks for atmosphere and its steaks and ribs

USA TODAY
The best in U.S. family restaurants

By Arlene Vigoda
USA TODAY

Which of the USA's largest family restaurant chains offer the tastiest experiences?

Southern-based Cracker Barrel, Western-based Stuart Anderson's and the Olive Garden, says a reader survey in *Consumer Reports'* June issue, on newsstands today.

Some 98,000 readers rated 36 casual eatery chains for quality of food, service, atmosphere and cost, based on a 100-point scale. None of the chains scored higher than 75.

People will "spend a few extra bucks for ambience and service, which you can't get at fast food places," says *Consumer Reports'* Tod Marks.

Among the results:

▷ **Family restaurants.** Top three: Cracker Barrel (75), Bob Evans (69) and Po-Folks (65). Cracker Barrel, with 120 outlets, "serves real good food with great prices," says Marks.

▷ **Steak/buffet houses.** Top three: Mr. Steak (64), Ryan's (64) and Golden Corral (63). Mr. Steak, with 60 outlets, has added lighter entrees and huge buffet-style food bars.

▷ **Casual dinner houses.** Top three: Stuart Anderson's (71), Olive Garden (70) and Steak and Ale (69). Stuart Anderson's, with 89 outlets, won high marks for atmosphere and its steaks and ribs.

Do You Want Some Good News?

The restaurant employment rate has fast surpassed total U.S. employment rate. As I write this, restaurant sales reached a record high of $45.9 billion in April of 2013.

As the recession continues to recover, people are becoming less frugal. Sales to baby boomers have gone up 6%.

Dream BIG!

Restaurants offer customers a valuable service and create jobs, with the real possibility of financial independence for the operator and family

Young people work at restaurants in high numbers to gain experience and earn money through high school and college. In the summer of 2013 alone, California businesses hired 41,700 restaurant workers. I can't tell you how many people have told me I helped put them or their children through college. I guess you could say that what we do is a tremendous contribution to the overall intelligence of the nation!

There's one other benefit coming out of the restaurant business but you'll have to ponder this one: By supporting restaurants you help slow down the increasing divorce rate. I bet you can figure this out.

If restaurants are commonly known to be risky ventures, why do banks disburse so many loans to them? In the past decade, more government-guaranteed loans have gone to full-service restaurants than any other industry, 34,138 in 2011 to be exact. The limited-service restaurant industry came in second with 25,288 loans.

One explanation for the high loan volume is the sheer number of diners and drive-ins and dinner houses. The National

Restaurant Association (NRA) recently reported that food service is the second-largest private industry in the Nation after health care.

The food service industry is number one in the nation and health care isn't really comparable as there is so much government involvement, insurance, politics and little retail and/or service business. (*This opinion courtesy of S. Anderson Review Board.*)

Now don't drop your book, this is not going to be full of statistics. And hey, since the restaurant business is dynamic and forever changing, it is not boring!

Every day, hundreds of restaurants become a vital part of not just the community but the entire national economy. I feel the industry has been unfairly criticized for the failure rate but let me assure you: being your own boss added to the glamorous nature of the business will offset the negatives and make the expenditure of time, energy and money well worthwhile.

The failure rate is actually no greater than the cross-industry average for all new businesses, according to statistics from the Small Business Administration and the Bureau of Labor Statistics. I know, I know … I promised no more statistics so, for now, let's leave this chapter while everyone's still in good spirits!

Since there is no longer a Stuart Anderson chain of restaurants, the following is not personal … but I am promoting all restaurants. Support local restaurants; they do so much for our country's economy.

TIP: If you gain a little weight
from all that eating, just hang around with fat
people and you'll feel much better.

Social Life: Willing to talk and engage in activities with other people; friendly, needing companionship; relating to or designed for activities in which people meet each other for pleasure.

Chapter 3

Where did all my Friends Go?

Fuggetaboutit! If you choose to be in this business, when five o'clock comes around and your friends are getting off the job, you're at work and when you get off work at ten or midnight, your friends are going home or to bed. Even the kids who are working in a restaurant part time to help with school expenses have to consider this. I don't like to get into negatives because I'm a positive kind of guy, but I think it's only right that I discuss it with you especially since it's not talked about enough.

The restaurant business will affect your life. Think about your family and good friends. Your life style as you now know it will be changed: One third of restaurant closings happen for this reason.

In the old Seattle days, before I got into the restaurant business, I remember meeting my friends after work. We went to cocktail parties or the movies and it was fun just to go out with the gang. Sometimes we'd splurge on glamorous restaurants like *Top of the Town, Victor Rossellini's 410 or 610,* or *Jim Ward's El Gaucho.* We always had a few laughs, at least a couple of martinis, (not necessarily in that order) and then got home at a reasonable hour. Those friendships meant a great deal to me. You know, most of us don't see our friends often enough as it is, let alone adding the time a restaurant career demands.

It's unavoidable: you will miss some good times with those old friends unless they come to see you. Because of the hours

"My social life!"

involved, there's little chance for a movie or a dinner date with the people who are an important part of your life. You don't get regular doses of their gossip or their laughter ... which can have a significant effect on relationships. It's a situation you have to get used to.

I experienced this dramatically over the years. We opened over 130 restaurants and I personally attended almost all of these events which meant travel all over the country. Since the restaurants were company owned and not franchises, they required more time, dedication and personal attention.

We usually arrived a few days before and stayed a couple of days after an opening. This demanding schedule was hard on my marriages to two good women and is probably why both ended in divorce. It also took me away from the buddies I'd had from high school and college.

Because I always seemed to be on the road, my two young daughters hardly recognized me and wanted to know who the strange man was. As they got older, they grew jealous of the business because it took up most of my time. Thankfully, today they are both beautiful daughters and the exes are still wonderful women and I'm sorry that my social life (or lack of same, depending on how you look at it), interfered with our lives. Hopefully, now that I'm over 90 years old, all is forgiven.

Eventually there is a light at the end of the tunnel: you start meeting and mixing with an entirely new group of people, some of whom are the vendors and customers you become acquainted with during your slower times. I found myself pulled toward the ones who were happy and smiled a lot.

I got to know a lot of quality people in the business and I wasn't the only one. Many of our employees found their future spouses at work or made lifelong friendships. It takes a little time but eventually you'll enjoy your new situation.

Out with the old, in with the gold!

Of all the gin joints in all the towns in the West, she had to walk into mine.

It was back in the early days ... I swear, someone had me in mind when Helen was created because she's the best thing that ever happened to me. As a truly wise individual once said, "I love being married; it's so great to find that one person you get to annoy for the rest of your life."

Actually, my VP of operations and I were looking for a top-notch right hand and couldn't find one we agreed on. Then, when a friend of our personnel director talked up a talented gal he knew, he in turn called Helen and persuaded her into coming in for an interview. She already had a good position working for the CEO of a computer manufacturing company and saw no reason to leave. But somehow we convinced her to join our team.

Helen has often said that as soon as she walked through the door, she could feel the camaraderie and knew this would be a great fit for her personality. Let's just say I'm glad she felt that way.

I'm reminded of the story of a gentleman advising a young man to "Find one who cooks, never mind the looks." Well, I found one who cooks and also has the looks. She can cook as if she

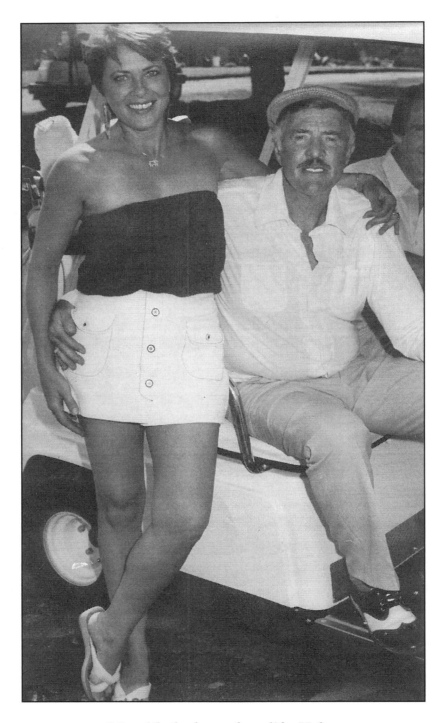

Me with the love of my life: Helen.

were on the side of the angels. Of course, most everything she knows she learned from me. (Well, maybe a couple of things.)

She does have one questionable habit, and let's see if I can tell this without getting into too much trouble. For years, I've called Helen "the daughter of Waste King." If I don't guard my plate with great care, she unashamedly attacks it. She's been known to go after our friends' and relatives' meals, also with fork in hand. To my knowledge, she has not made any moves on a stranger yet, but I watch her closely.

When we eat at home, Helen doesn't usually display much of an appetite and eats a lot less than when we go out. This means she is less likely to go after my plate. One night, as I watched my evening news and fondled the remote, I noticed in the reflection of the window my wife cooking AND EATING. After observing this over several nights, I asked, "Are you eating without me?" The quick reply between bites was, "No, I have to sample the cooking to be sure it's just right for you!"

Yeah, right!

She really does the taste thing to extreme.

Even with her healthy appetite, Helen manages to keep a great figure. She does this by eating a balanced diet and doesn't seem tempted by my weakness for desserts or sweets. For that, I both pity and envy her. I always have a yearning for these creations with a special appreciation of anything chocolate. Maybe the fact that Helen is allergic to chocolate helps her say no. And, yes, to protect my dessert plate, I order anything I can with chocolate in it.

When Helen and I were working and traveling together, I discovered how nice it was to be able to share the business with someone who cared and understood. Despite the fight for food, she opened up a new social life for me that was bolstered by her charm and intelligence. We started to pick up with friendly people, happy people, new people and younger people.

As we continued working together, things did change. She gradually and steadily became the love of my life and the heart of my business. She brought her son Mike, many friends and a whole big family with her as she was one of eight kids.

I think I became easier to get along with because of the fun the two of us were enjoying and creating. We got to know some great customers and became closer to the crews. The busy,

busy times became more fun because we could share those times. We could enjoy the people more and I think they enjoyed us more. My social life was back, even better than before and I was tickled to death.

All the people who worked with us shared our happier attitudes; it was contagious. Our good times filtered down to the vice presidents, managers, chefs and all the way through. Over time, we became very active and our contentment was felt by the customers as well.

Of course, some restaurants are totally operated by a family, with one taking up chef duties in the kitchen, one bartending, one out front greeting and the others prepping and serving or whatever else is needed. In this set-up, the whole family can enjoy a rich social life while working.

**TIP: Always remember, it's hard
to fire a member of your family without
causing hard feelings.**

**TIP: Hiring a good manager you
can trust is key so you don't
have to be on site every hour of every day.**

But for everyone else, the truth is that your social life will change. There's no way around it; it's a significant fact of the business and one not usually discussed – at least not in any books I've read. I feel it should be stressed more so you can prepare yourself for it. Just remember to remain positive because you have the opportunity for an amazingly rewarding life ahead of you.

Chapter 4

In a New York Minute

I've always enjoyed reading biographies and autobiographies but I do have two long-standing objections: There is too much emphasis on childhood and early adolescence. Experts tell us the formative years are what shape a person. Fine, it may be true. But I generally skim or skip the early chapters and jump to the era that makes a particular person qualified to be the subject of a book.

The second objection, and a real pain in the ass, is the sexual conquests attributed to some sports figure or movie star. They're usually repetitious and by the dozen. I really can do without the mattress surfing.

When I first started in business I lied about being older and grew a mustache to drum up a little respect. Later, when I lived on the ranch, I lied the other way around but kept the mustache. We often gave hay rides around the upper part of the ranch to groups of senior citizens, high-school graduates, business people and so forth. I asked the fellows driving the people around how the passengers liked the ride and what caught their interest. They all agreed there were three universal questions:

1. "How many cattle are on the ranch?"

(This is like asking you how much money you have in the bank.)

2. "How many acres make up the ranch?"

(See the note above.)

3. "How old is Stuart Anderson?"

For some reason, senior citizens especially wanted to know my age. I don't understand why that should matter to people but truth is, I lied so often even I got confused. And when I did, I could always fall back on one interesting little fact. I was born in and on the exact year, month, and day the tomb of Egyptian King Tutankhamen was opened, still considered the greatest archeological accomplishment of all time.

After being enclosed for more than three millennia, the tomb's unveiling was supervised by archeologists Lord Carnarvon and Howard Carter, who oversaw letting out 3000 years of stale air. When I first learned this, I asked my mother, "Do you suppose, since the opening was the exact time of my birth, that I might be . . . ?"

When I saw the "like-I-gave-birth-to-this-child" expression on her face I dropped the subject and never brought it up again. Just as well that I leave it alone; there is that curse of King Tut, you know.

When I write or talk about my early years, I'd like to make them full of drama and danger. Unfortunately, no drama; no danger. My childhood was a nearly perfect Norman Rockwell-type of existence. At least for me. I did give my folks some grief.

For example, I attended three high schools even though my folks never moved. That's got to tell you something! I was the kind of kid my mother told me not to play with. We lived in Broadmoor in Seattle, an exclusive enclave with a private golf course. In a way, I regret not suffering the pangs of the Depression. I don't mean to trivialize it to those who struggled through it; however, I did have to walk clear across the golf course to go back and forth to school each day.

My father never worked at home. He never cooked or washed the dishes. He never mowed the lawn or cleaned the windows, nor did he play golf or go fishing. He was a physician who practiced medicine day and night. The way he lived his life taught me that when you love what you do, it's not work.

He became world famous in his field of orthopedic surgery and because he was always looking for a better way to help his patients, he invented and held patents on orthopedic operating tables, leg splints and casts. He was at his peak earning ability during the Depression. Consequently, instead of suffering as so many others were, we had maids waiting on us, and two Cadillacs in the garage.

Seated: my mother, Susan, and father, Dr. Roger Anderson.
Laying down: our dog Tippy.
Standing left to right, the three angels: me, sister Suzanne and brother Roger (Two out of three ain't bad.)
We're looking at our dog like he's going to attack the photographer.

I remember he used to ask my brother and me for the very latest jokes so he could use them in the speeches he gave around the country. I attended a couple of these lectures, and when he came to the story we'd given him, why I'd hardly recognize it. I never remember a joke, much less tell it well, but compared to Dr. Roger Anderson, I was hilarious. He understood what was funny about what he was saying but his timing was terrible. I used to sink down in my chair with embarrassment when he tried to be funny.

While we were growing up and long after, my brother and I were always known as Dr. Roger's sons and lived in the shadow of his fame. I remember people often commenting: "Oh, that's Stuey; he's one of Dr. Roger's kids." So, I couldn't have been more pleased when, two months before he passed away, he told me he was proud to be known as Stuart Anderson's father.

One time, my father took the train from St. Paul, Minnesota, to Fort Dodge, Iowa, to see his granddaughter a few days after her birth. Earlier that day, he'd been in St. Paul to bury his father. It was unlike his nature to be expressive but I could hear he was more than emotional as he said, "I've just seen one life leave this earth and now I get to see a new life come in."

Twenty-some years later, my first-born spoke eloquently at my father's funeral, a hard task for anyone. I miss my father; he had a life that worked.

My daughters inherited great longevity genes. When the first one was born, she had seven great-grandparents – and I was twenty-six when I married, which was considered late in those days. When my second daughter was born about five years later, she had one great-grandparent.

After my stint in Patton's Army and an additional year at the University of Washington, I went to Fort Dodge, Iowa, to help my grandfather, Dr. W. F. Carver, manage his office building, an eight-story structure with mostly professional offices. In the first three months, I more than doubled the rental income, which did not make me a lot of new friends! My grandfather was so good-hearted, he couldn't bear to raise the rent despite raging inflation. Obviously, I didn't take after him.

**Four generations: My mother, daughter Christopher
holding her second son Logan and me.**

I had recently married Marilyn Smith in Boise, Idaho, and after the ceremony, we moved directly to Fort Dodge, so it was a honeymoon town where we found new friends. The tenants weren't crazy about me but I was young enough not to give a damn. Also, my first daughter was born there, so I have fond memories of the place ... and I surely learned a few lessons during that period.

**TIP: Don't anticipate
the quirks of human nature.**

My grandfather's building had two elevators and three "boys" to keep them operating. I figured I could cut expenses tremendously by making the elevators automatic, which was a fairly new innovation and going strong in the big cities. Naturally the elevator operators had to go.

Whenever visitors pressed the button to open the doors and no attendant was there to greet them, they didn't get in. They stood there wondering what to do next until finally deciding to wait for the next elevator where they discovered the same empty space – no attendant. Some of the better-traveled people understood the new-fangled lifts, but too many of the country folks coming in to see their doctor or dentist turned around, found the stairs, and walked up to their floor. I wound up having to hire back an operator for one of the elevators so everyone could conveniently get to the upper floors.

Eventually, both elevators became fully automatic but it took a couple of years and they didn't pay for themselves as quickly as I'd planned. I will say this lesson helped me anticipate customers' reactions in later years as a restaurateur.

Then came my next great move. There was some extra space in the lobby, so I installed a cigar stand with all the usual accompaniments. Smart move! It included a Coke machine I'd decided to buy instead of lease. Later, when I took a pencil to that brilliant decision, I figured it would take me 21 years to pay for it.

Fool me once, shame on you; fool me twice, shame on me. Yes, I did it again.

I bought chocolates for the holiday season by the ton at a great price and stored the boxes behind the elevator shafts. I didn't realize that the elevators would create enough heat to melt all the chocolate. It smelled good for a while, a small consolation and that lingering, sweet odor became a bitter reminder of my goof.

On my days off, I loved driving out to the farms around Fort Dodge, what I like to call the buckle on the corn belt. The farms were (and still are) well groomed and very productive, with numerous cattle in excellent shape. My grandparents were doing all right, thanks to the income generated by the increased rent, and I was inspired by the beauty of the land, so I decided to go back west and become a rancher. I knew I wasn't going to make it selling chocolates!

**Grandson Will's Wedding to Beautiful Tracy Higgens,
September 2012. Helen, Stuart, Daughter Quincy & husband Ken,
"The Happy Couple," grandson Logan,
Daughter Christopher and her husband David.**

"MOTHER, LET YOUR BOY GO!"

Chapter 5

Our Ends are in our Beginnings

I'm the type of guy who likes to forget the wrong turns I've made in life, not to mention the dumb decisions. However, the next move I made, as common as it is dumb, I'll always recall with a smile.

I had served my country in the Army, gotten some business experience under my belt, got married and welcomed my first-born child. After my Iowa adventures, I headed back to Seattle, wife and child in tow, to start a new chapter. We ended up moving in with "Mummy and Daddy" with all this baggage. They had a beautiful home on the shores of Lake Washington and I felt right at home. No rent, the food was good, and it wasn't costing anything.

Made sense to me.

I began looking for work but it was summer and I wasn't in any big hurry. My baby daughter had just started to walk and soon she was running all over the house. She was one of those babies who could never sit still and I enjoyed watching her. Life was good. I had it made. Was this great or what?

Actually, it was an "or what." How I remember my father telling me, "No matter how large the house, it's never big enough for two mistresses." I was really pushing the envelope and he was never one to let me get away with anything, so . . .

I went gently into that good night.

With my Army savings, I secured both a job and a place to live via one crazy move by leasing a small hotel in downtown

Seattle with ninety ugly rooms, one of which was ours. It was called the Caledonia and was located at Seventh and Union. What a dump! It made the Bates Motel look like the Waldorf-Astoria. (I'm not hurting anyone's feelings; the old building died and the site now lies ten feet under the freeway.)

I handled the front desk and switchboard on the graveyard shift because I couldn't get anyone to work those hours in that neighborhood. Out of sheer boredom, I played a lot of pinball in the lobby. Although few people walking by chose to stay at the Caledonia, I did get some business from cab drops. It worked this way: When a cabby picked up a passenger who was looking for a reasonably priced place to stay, he'd take the fare to my "palace," drive off, then sneak back to retrieve his dollar kickback. I paid out quite a few dollars every night. Of course, sometimes the fare wouldn't like the room (can you blame them?) and I'd be out all the way around. Other times I got lucky and the bellhop would tip me off that the guests were coming back down to the desk for a refund.

In a New York second, I was very hard to find.

Included in the master lease was a small cafe which was, décor-wise, the perfect match for my dumpy rooms. For months, the tenant hadn't paid the rent so I reluctantly took over the operation and that's how I stumbled onto my lifetime career. All at once, I was the proprietor of the Caledonia Grill. Too bad the bus station counter was the only competition worse than mine.

But suddenly, I got lucky! The voters had recently approved the sale of liquor in Washington state and hotels were given licensing preference. As fast as I could, I installed a small bar in the cavernous lobby and immediately turned a brisk business from hookers, seamen, hustlers, and wrestlers. Although it was a very tough area and the opposite environment to which I was accustomed, I actually found it fascinating to work and mingle with my patrons, so many of whom lived on the fringe.

Most of these folks were constantly working angles or scheming something. But I soon discovered that the hookers, who normally worked out of houses in Alaska, were simply in Seattle for R&R. As regular as rain, as soon as the fishing season ended, there they'd be.

They were great gals and I learned a lot from them – and we're not talking about sex either. You couldn't find a phony bone in their bodies. They were always up front, full of humor and loved to tease me.

The people who sustained me in those crucial early years had few breaks in life but they made the best of them. I'm certainly not ashamed of my humble business beginnings – everyone has to start somewhere. It wasn't as if I'd sold my soul to the devil – but it was a life of seedy hotels, smoky bars, and blatant, blameless sex.

TIP: Gimmicks are great salesmanship but use them with good taste. Get to know your local area and who your customers are.

Since I couldn't name the bar "Hookers' Hangout," I called it "The Ringside Room" to entice the wrestlers and their followers from the Eagles' Auditorium across the street. Wrestling was just starting to be SHOW TIME.

I also installed a heavy hawser, which is a thick rope, instead of a normal bar rail. I recall one seaman who came in from an Alaskan tour. He loosened his belt, tied it around that huge rope and announced he was there to do some heavy drinking.

That's one way to tie one on – pun intended.

Then there was the day my Mother came to visit her "little boy." She was very much a lady and had to overcome her embarrassment at being seen in such a lowlife area.

The bar was so small you had to squeeze by one of the stools to get to the other end. As my mother inched forward, she brushed up against the stool's occupant, a wrestler, who grabbed for his wallet and yelled, "Hey, watch it, sister!"

She turned bright red and that was her last visit to the dump.

In those early years, there were "Blue Laws" in Washington State. For example, women couldn't sit at the bar, period. No

The Caledonia entry.

one, male or female, could carry a drink while walking around – they had to be seated. Federal law prohibited us from serving Indians.

I ask you, can you always tell an Indian from a part-Indian from a non-Indian? It wasn't easy and I tried to give my guests the benefit of the doubt for both our sakes. I don't know why but I never did get in trouble for it.

On Sundays we couldn't serve liquor at all, which meant we had to close Saturday at midnight. This last rule usually meant shutting down a full house and at times, I'd almost cry.

I remember paying wages every week on Friday at six o'clock, the time the banks closed. I'm sure that routine created some hardships for my employees but I needed the weekend business to cover those checks. When they requested their pay early, I told them, "No, no, no, sorry!" I couldn't tell them there was no money in the bank ... they might've felt nervous and looked for work elsewhere.

In fact, there were times cash was so tight I even tried banking out of town to gain time on mail transfers. Of course, that wouldn't work today with electronic deposit and withdrawal. One thing you can be sure of: whatever the transaction, if the interest is in the bank's favor it'll be immediate but if the interest is in your favor, it might take a while.

There was another economical move I'll discuss that I did not particularly enjoy and that I wasn't very good at. I had to take care of the bar before the lunch shift until a real bartender came aboard. It was only a couple of hours in the morning but I've always been morning-impaired. One incident in particular made that abundantly clear.

Jim Greco was an architect from the firm of Bystrom and Greco who did a great deal of work for me on the early restaurants. (Arnie Bystrom eventually worked on my seafood venture, Stuart's at Shilshole and it is still going strong but under the ownership of Anthony's.)

Anyhow, Jim Greco strolled into the bar just before lunch. After I had greeted and served him, he muttered something I did not quite catch. It was kind of like an "Oh damn," but I wasn't ready for that so I pretended to be really busy to avoid talking to him.

Although he was clear down at the bar's far end, I could still tell he was grousing about something. It is a known fact that bartenders are obliged to listen to a patron's trials and tribulations – but not me, if I can help it.

Now here was Jim, groaning again, a good friend and customer not to mention important to our design work. Finally, I felt guilty enough to hear him out. I dragged myself down to his end of the bar, took a deep breath and marshaled the strength to ask, "Okay, okay, it sorta sounds like you've got a problem, so let's hear it! What is it? I'm listening."

He never missed a beat. "Well, I'll tell you what, Stuart," he spit out, "it's none of your damn business!"

That's just one of a thousand such stories in this crazy business.

It was also because of my money situation that I kept one of the lowest inventories in town. Whenever we ran out of slower-moving liquor, I'd have to send the bartender to the Washington State Liquor Store up the street to purchase a bottle at retail prices. Then, as now, you could only buy your booze through state-run stores using cash or certified check.

Occasionally, the local liquor inspector would show up unannounced to make sure all bottles had the proper stamps on them. I didn't like the guy so I'd always try to get rid of him in a hurry, insisting I was too busy right then. "Don't let the door hit you in the ass on your way out," I'd mumble under my breath.

When I first met the inspector, he'd told me in a sly sort of way that he'd like to have enough money to buy a new hat every month. When I asked him why he needed so many hats, he gave me a disgusted look and walked away. That's why he deserved to have that door hit him on the way out. He must've figured I was the dumbest bar operator on his beat and maybe I was, but I never bought anyone a hat.

In the early fifties in Seattle, kickbacks were an accepted practice. No one would even suggest such a thing now, I'm sure. But here I am, winding down some old cow path and losing focus, so let me get back to where I was.

With the start of the Korean War, Seattle became a boom town because, being a port city, there was a constant flow of servicemen and ships in and out. It wasn't unusual for my hotel to enjoy up to a hundred and fifteen percent occupancy rate. These were loose times and I felt like putting up a sign: "PLEASE RE-MEMBER THE NAME UNDER WHICH YOU REGISTERED."

The good news was that the robust cash flow finally allowed me to make some improvements. I moved the lobby to where the dumpy cafe had been and relocated the dining room to the large lobby space. I named it "The French Quarter" and changed the lounge name to "The Downbeat Room," removing the famous rope rail in the process. At last, I was a real restaurateur!

As this was in the early fifties, when stereo music was just coming of age, I placed two huge speakers at opposite ends of the lounge that could simulate the sound of a train running right through the bar – or so it seemed on those great demonstration cassette tapes that came with the systems. Talk about a gimmick! The customers flocked to hear it.

Bill Teeter, an early associate and a well-known interior designer, went with me to the Salvation Army to pick up old musical instruments (if they didn't play, all the better). To flesh out our Downbeat theme, Bill hung them all over the back of the bar in an artistic design.

With the state-of-the-art music capability and a slightly more fashionable dining area, the new layout brought in a different clientele.

Feeling uncomfortable, the hookers and wrestlers moved on.

I miss those teachers of life and wish them well wherever they might be.

We have lost Bill Teeter (Del-Teet Furniture) as well as my buddy, Hughie, who's part of the story I'm about to tell. Both died far too early of cancer, leaving the world a little less bright.

I needed a bartender to go with the new setup. Hugh Klopfenstein (of family-owned Klopfenstein's, an up-scale clothing store), was an old friend and future roommate after my first divorce. He got around town a lot, so I asked him to find me a new bartender.

That's how I came to hire Bruce Attebery, who eventually became Black Angus' senior vice president. I checked him out at the tavern where he worked: young, barefoot, six-foot nine-inches tall and singing along with the jukebox ... my kind of guy! Everything fit except the feet. He'd have to find some size-fourteen shoes and put 'em on.

Bruce was a great bartender and continued his sing-along with Frank Sinatra and other old favorites on that wonderful sound system of ours. We did have one real conflict, though. One September, I started a promotion running a bus to the University of Washington football games with dinner and drinks. I asked Bruce to knock off the regular music on home-game Saturdays and play all the football fight songs instead. All Saturday long, while the revelers were there, we listened to "Bow Down to Washington," "Fight, Fight, Fight, for Washington State," and other ditties. Bruce still wanted to whoop it up with

Frankie. "Sorry," I told him, "but we've got to get into the old football spirit."

When the last game of the season came, as the bus was getting ready to leave, I told Bruce he wouldn't have to play the records any longer. You'd think I'd unchained a monster. I heard later that he'd emptied the jukebox of all my beautiful records, took them out into the street, and used them for Frisbees, shouting obscenities with each toss. I didn't want to be there after the laughter stopped; some clean-up job!

You might be wondering: Did this boy/man really become the senior vice president of the entire Stuart Anderson Restaurant chain? Yes. Most everyone changes as they mature and Bruce was very instrumental in the growth of the company.

At last, we had everything going in the lounge except a little sex appeal. I don't remember how, but I got hold of (not literally) two tall blondes ... and I mean TALL, with legs up to their eye sockets ... as servers. Now we had more than a little sex appeal. Those gorgeous women, named oddly enough, Sam and Jerri, became legends. With a wardrobe of the first micro-mini-skirts in Seattle, these big girls combined with the big bartender and the big speakers made quite a splash. I was making it big!

I can't believe I forgot to tell you about the food. At first I tried a French menu featuring escargot and a lot of other fancy dishes I've forgotten the names of but it didn't go over. The area and the building had been in the dumps for too long a time for that menu to work. One Saturday night, I had a grand total of nine people at the height of the dinner hour with five of them being family ... well, that tells you something.

I often have to learn things the hard way but I'm quick to adjust.

It took about two months with the French menu before trying a $1.95 steak dinner.

WHOA!

That's right:$1.95. The steaks were cut small, shipped in from Australia and probably wouldn't rate a "good" under our grading system today. Although this was a dramatic change, it was not an unusual menu for the time except for the price. Why reinvent the wheel? No sir; no pioneer me! I always considered a pioneer as a man with an ass full of arrows.

Now that both the lounge and dining room were starting to get some patronage, I had even more cash available. That's when I bought into a farm in Redmond, Washington with my friend, Fred McGuire, who had recently come into an inheritance.

My longed-for ranching experience was really beginning!

The acreage had a small packing house on it and the meat I was getting off this property made the steaks coming out of Australia look like pieces of cardboard. The imported beef had to be tenderized and if we didn't soak it enough, you'd swear you were eating leather. If the Aussie steaks were left in the liquid too long, it would fall off the fork before you could get it to your mouth.

It was enough to turn you into a vegetarian.

I realized I had to switch to all-choice steak born and bred in the good old U.S. of A. and raise the price accordingly. The increase (to $2.95) was large enough to require a leap of faith and it took me years to live down a reputation for serving imported commercial meat, which I did just short of a year. To this day there are a small number of people who will tell you the Black Angus restaurants served tenderized or imported Australian beef. Not true! I wonder if this mistaken idea about Stuart Anderson's steaks endured because our original price was well below the competition's, even after we started serving "choice."

Thank heaven the bar sales helped offset the high food cost. Even so, to maintain my pricing and make a profit, I had to "turn tables" three times or more per night – that is, serve three different groups at the same table over an evening, not an easy feat. We took no reservations, a smart strategy that created a constant waiting line.

We also had one-plate service, a limited dessert menu and no highchairs, all of which helped further shorten the time-per-meal. Lose the kids and save valuable table space.

Was I a meanie?

Moving on ...

Chapter 6

It's a Barnum & Bailey World

When the Seattle World's Fair closed in 1962, and in spite of a lull in the economy, I was looking to expand and take my format and gimmicks with me. In short order, I found a shuttered restaurant building and talked financing with an eager landlord. His name was Bayard McIntosh and he became a good friend. I told him I had a sound business formula but that I needed some financing. I also explained that with my low prices and profit margins, I couldn't afford to pay a percentage type of rent, the usual practice in those days.

I'd like to think I took after the structure of J. C. Penney, Walmart, or Woolworth's Five and Dime. They were all high volume/low margin concerns, leaving little room for this type of rent. My food costs alone hovered around fifty percent, far exceeding the norm.

With the one-plate service and highly competent people who could handle five or six tables at a time, I had considerably lightened the labor costs. But there was no question that rent, along with other occupancy expenditures, had to remain reasonable to make the plan succeed.

The location I scouted had once been the site of a famous Seattle restaurant called "Skipper's" and I remember being a customer when I was in high school. After the Korean War, it had fallen on hard times and changed hands twice. The last operators were Asians who called the place the "Double Joy" until they had to close the door. The building sat unused for months, and there's absolutely nothing worse than an empty restaurant that hasn't been scrubbed clean.

Chock full of disgusting rats, putrid smells and bugs of all kinds, you'd hear the scurrying of tiny feet the moment you opened the door and turned on the lights. If my future customers had seen how we started out, I don't believe they'd have ever come through those doors.

Before I could even start a major clean-up and remodel, I had to obtain a liquor license. Some dweeb on the liquor board (it's just as well I don't remember his name) said he couldn't grant me a license because, if Asians and their family members couldn't make it, I certainly couldn't. I rounded up an attorney and the landlord and we went to the state capitol in Olympia to plead our case before the entire Liquor Control Board. That one member continued mouthing stupidities about Asians in the restaurant business that had nothing to do with anything but we made our case, which was a good one, and got our license.

On April Fools' Day of 1964, we turned on the sign, unlocked the door and got out of the way. The first Stuart Anderson's Black Angus was open! Our selection of six different cuts of choice steak all at the same price of $2.95 was an immediate hit, especially since it included a full dinner with all the fixings. People had never seen this kind of price point for beef and it became so popular, customers waited in line an hour or more to be seated and served. Thankfully, that never stopped them from coming and that line stayed with us, giving us a tremendous advantage in turning the tables even as we expanded into other cities.

The setup proved interesting in an unexpected way: that waiting line created a place for games, tricks, stories, and human reactions of all kinds. (I hope you don't recognize yourself in what's coming, although most of us will.)

Some people felt that if they went into the lounge, they wouldn't be seated as quickly. Not true! Some believed if they sat close to the name-taker and stared at him or her, they'd get in faster. Not true! Then there were those who felt that if they got up and asked every five minutes where they were on the list, it'd help get them get in sooner. Not true!

The first Black Angus-1964.

We honored that list like it was written in stone no matter who you were, with one exception – me! Well, and maybe the President of The United States.

One night when a male customer was told it'd be an hour wait, he glared at the hostess and asked indignantly, "Do you know who I am?" She quietly answered, "No sir." When he proudly proclaimed, "I'm Stuart Anderson!" she quickly replied, "It will still be an hour wait, sir."

The hostess was my daughter, Quincy.

Over the years of working with a waiting list, you become an expert on human behavior and start to instinctively recognize a person's status. Say there's a couple sitting in the bar looking straight ahead, rarely speaking, and when they do, they're certainly not looking at each other. They appear rather unhappy, especially the man for some reason. They want to be called to dinner NOW. Couple Number One consists of two spouses married to the wrong people.

Then there's Couple Number Two, who can't get enough of each other. They don't look at anything or anyone else and could not care less about when they're called. You can spot that familiar expression that says, "Is it going to happen tonight?" You would love to move them down the list and move Couple Number One up.

Sorry, the list is inviolable.

Couple Number Three looks nervous. Perhaps they're on a blind date. They don't recognize the name when it's called, so you have to repeat it two or three times.

Some people actually memorized two or three names above their own and when those names were called, they made sure theirs was next. Others insisted on looking at the list even when it was upside down to them.

TIP: Just a word to those who might be anxious: don't be discouraged by the list or turned off by the amount of time a restaurant host is estimating. Most people in charge will quote you a time that is longer than actually expected to alleviate some of the pressure and complaints.

Not that it matters much anymore, since reservations generally are taken now that the marketplace has become more competitive.

When we opened the second Black Angus in Tacoma, we had the usual crush of opening week trade. The store manager, Bruce Attebery, who you've met, had his first experience in working with a waiting list and came upon what seemed at first glance like a great solution.

Guests often arrived in twos more often than in fours and many of our restaurants didn't have enough two-tops (tables for two) but did have plenty of four-tops. Bruce went down the line asking each twosome whether they'd like to meet their neighbors by making it a foursome.

What are they going to say with the other couple right behind them and six-foot, nine-inch boss waving a clipboard in their faces? "No thanks?"

To his credit, Bruce managed to fill all those four-tops, and because the volume of business meant more dough in the cash register, I thought it was a great idea. However, on the drive home I started to wise up. Those people who'd been put on the spot wouldn't be coming back.

And to all the people from Tacoma who said, "You folks will never make it in that spot!" I have this to say: "Good call!" That particular store is no longer in operation. It had no parking and was in a lousy location.

TIP: Parking is critical in most cities. Believe it!

Right now, I can hear you all asking again: This guy Bruce Attebery; he really became your senior vice president?"

"Yes," I say, "and a damn good one!"

One last story and I'll mosey along. My sister almost never took advantage of her relationship to me in any of the restaurants. That being said, on the way home from a ski weekend, she realized she was running late to meet the baby sitter. When she told the maître d' that she was my sister and couldn't wait the thirty minutes, he said, "Yo, sure," before turning to a co-worker. "Hey Ed," he said with a smirk, "we've got another one of Stuart's sisters here." Then he admonished my sister, "Back to the end of the line, please."

After hearing this story, I broke down and gave her a card that read, "This is my only sister."

Soon after, she had occasion to try it again. When she gave the card to the name-taker, he gave it to the maître d' who loudly proclaimed, "Hey, look! This lady is really enterprising and she should really get somewhere for her effort ... how about the end of the line, miss!"

I got this report later and frankly, I was pleased that the wait list had been honored ... it was and still is an important image to maintain. Of course, I never told my sister so!

One time, while talking on the phone, my brother and I were both wondering how we got to be first in line when they gave out sisters. How did we earn that? I sure do miss them both.

Chapter 7

Bar Stool Stu

There came a time in the early development of this chain when some of my practices had a slightly sinister cast. In the accompanying picture, you'll notice what appears to be a vulture sitting on the shelf above my head. That's exactly what it represents and was given to me by my cohort in picking up dead and dying restaurants, my attorney and friend in the early days, Dick Dameyer.

So yes, these business practices had a dark side but, conversely, a glimmer of hope for someone's dying dream. Here's how it worked: I was in contact with and "romancing" the credit manager of the large restaurant supply house that sold me my barstools. When his company had to repo a restaurant's tables or chairs because of a default on payments, I was already perched to swoop in exactly like a vulture.

At one point, they'd come close to picking up MY barstools but I'd gotten a secondary loan for added protection, something you could do in those days that would be impossible today.

As I got to know the restaurant supply people better, I learned some tricks about failing restaurants and soon earned the nicknamed Barstool Stu. They'd notify me in advance whenever they were going to a restaurant to pick up equipment and/or furniture so that I could check things out.

When I came across someone who was about to see his or her dreams flushed down the toilet, I offered an opportunity to salvage some dignity and maybe even come out with something.

**The vulture looking down on Helen
and me circa 1974.**

Was "Barstool Stu" picking up bones or giving someone on the skids a chance to start over somewhere else? You make the call.

A dead or dying restaurant is a sad thing to see. Advertising stops just when it's needed most, as does any thought of remodeling. When the deliveries start coming C.O.D., employees often become nervous or depressed and begin the sad process of looking for other jobs. It's a vicious circle.

This was the moment when I stepped in and started talking to all the parties involved, providing more hope than despair. I usually took over the lease so the restaurant operator didn't have to file for bankruptcy or suffer the indignity of repossessed furniture. And more often than not, the employees got to keep their jobs.

All my Good Wishes go to those Who Failed

And let's not forget the landlord through all this. He got excited about having a renter with a good reputation, even though he had to contribute some financing to help me remodel.

Finding these situations and diving down to take advantage of the injured, was I a Prince of Darkness in a black hat or a savior? Again, it's your call.

Before I entered into these vulture-style negotiations, I put together my "sophisticated" (or should I say simple?) marketing research from whatever sources I had available: Opening customer counts (number of customers per day counted by sales receipts); interviews with start-up employees; customer and ex-customer opinions; and food and bar sale percentages.

As the chain grew, Vice President of Development Ron Stephenson compiled comprehensive evaluations using spot-on negotiating skills and located many of the successful restaurant sites still operating today. Periodically, the two of us chartered a private airplane to visit locations and study the general area, including traffic flow trends and population densities. We usually took a fun group from the office along for support.

TIP: It was important for me to know if the
previous owners had ever enjoyed success.
If their restaurant had generated
a brisk business in the first month or two,
then their failure would more likely have
resulted from poor management.

This could be caused by the wrong pricing,
lousy food or service, kitchen stagnation,
and/or all those operational faults
that contribute to bad management, things
that were fixable.

For a while, Ron employed a service that gave us data on income, race, age, occupation, etc. within a one- to five-mile radius of our target. But even with all these statistics at hand, Ron relied on his gut feeling before making a decision and he insisted I do the same … asking for my blessing, of course, before any deal was finalized. This in-depth analysis was also applied to the many "build-to-suit" operations which were in our future. In that scenario, the property owner would lease us the land and either he or we would build the restaurant to our specifications.

It took me eight years – from 1964 to 1972 – to go from the first to the 12th Black Angus Restaurant. Financing was difficult and complicated to obtain with most of the funding coming from two sources. First and foremost were the landlords, who often contributed building improvements while delaying our rental payments. They couldn't have been more cooperative.

TIP: No one is more eager to do
business than smart owners
of empty buildings.

There was one rule I always observed in taking over a failing or a closed restaurant: I would change the exterior and interior appearance as much as possible, always with the landlords' participation. Because the time to deal with them is before you pay any rent or invest one single dime. Once you get your operation rolling, landlords are apt to become unavailable. I appreciated their involvement and I couldn't have done it without them.

The second investment source consisted of the food suppliers who had extended my long-term credit when I needed it most. Some really compassionate people can be found in the hospitality field and I made sure they were paid on the committed date even if I had to put a second contract on my furniture (which you could also do in those days).

There's an old adage in the hotel biz:

"If a room isn't sold for that night, its value is gone forever."

This can apply to a table in a restaurant:

"The most expensive item in a restaurant is an empty chair."

Should a person go into this fascinating business when they may have to stare at empty seats and hate doing it? Should you? Answer these questions:

1) Are you willing to work long hours?
2) Do you enjoy being around different kinds of people and lots of them?
3) Are you open-minded and tolerant?
4) Can you let go of your dream if it isn't working?
5) Can you hire smart and manage well?
6) Do you realize that to profit you must learn to please?

Always have a plan to do something differently, and if different doesn't work, plan something else. In any fast-paced enterprise, there's never enough time for the hard work necessary to build it up. Frankly, unless you're willing to adapt, you might very well run out of money even if you have a ton of it. The rule of thumb is to have enough money to be able to support a business for six months.

I attended a seminar once where the so-called expert insisted that hard work and more hard work was the only answer. Nonsense! Long hours, yes, but it better be fun because fun is contagious and, like a pebble tossed into a pond, the ripple effect reaches out affecting everything and everyone involved.

Hire carefully and delegate with confidence. It sounds so simple but it's powerful enough that there's more about this in the next chapter.

Of course, I can't forget the banks and their involvement in the financing of these early stores. I had notes with them but every one of those notes was co-signed by just about everybody … landlords or anyone else who was handy. Do I sound like I'm critical of bankers? Not really. If I were a banker, I might be nervous when a restaurant man came fishing for a loan.

The bank doesn't serve steaks and we don't cash checks!

That's the saying we used to hang over our registers. Times have changed, of course. I think both sides now violate these rules to some extent.

When we opened our third Black Angus in Spokane, Washington, we made every effort to divorce our operation from the highly competitive and therefore "accursed" sister city of Seattle. We banked locally and used every scheme we could think of to disguise the fact that our money went to Seattle. It was an exercise in futility. Besides, we found that our Spokane customers or customers from anywhere for that matter, don't give a hoot about where you came from as long as you gave them value for their hard-earned dollars.

Chapter 8

The Curtain Rises

I don't think our restaurant customers realize how much is involved or what goes on before the public arrives. Everyone has spent some time in a restaurant for lunch or dinner and I thank all of you. However, it's quite something else before that curtain rises. You'd be surprised at how different the atmosphere is from what you might expect.

The kitchen crew starts arriving between seven and nine a.m. You need a password to get in but I doubt you'd really care to enter. It's noisy! The radio's blasting rock 'n' roll, pots and pans are banging, someone's telling a joke, dishes and glasses are clicking and clinking; you can hardly hear the heavy-duty, commercial vacuum cleaner over all the other racket. The harsh working lights are blazing so brightly, you'd swear you were in a furniture warehouse that was on fire. The bartender is counting his opening cash till. It's fascinating to listen to the jokes, fun put-downs and teasing but you also know that everyone's watching the time.

The restaurant business is show business, more so than most others I know. Setting the stage properly is a major production, second only to the quality of the food. As the opening hour approaches, the tempo ramps up. The employees I barely recognized earlier hit the lockers and reappear decked out in their uniforms.

Back in the sixties, the uniforms our gals wore were provocative. I can't think of any one thing that gave us more grief

Some early advertising from Spokane, Washington.

than how these gals reacted, whether positively or negatively. At first we asked for feedback at our in-store meetings. BIG MISTAKE! It was like opening a floodgate. They couldn't agree among themselves. What looked good on this one over here looked lousy on someone else. It became an off-limit subject at all subsequent meetings.

Sally Johnson Newbury, who worked for me a long time and is still a friend, likes to tell a story on me and my uniforms.

"When I was interviewed for work at the French Quarter, Stuart held up what appeared to be two handkerchiefs and told me to go back to the dressing room and put them on. I about died, but I wanted the work, so I put the outfit on and returned to his office. He immediately said `Okay, you start at five o'clock.'"

This is obviously an exaggeration, but these gals were attractive by my standards and they had a great deal to do with increasing business. In the early sixties I could say "Hey, with that body you could go places!" and they would smile and thank me. Of course, I wouldn't dare say that today but sexist or not, those outfits did work their enchantment on me and many others.

Incidentally, I'm sure I've been "politically incorrect" a number of times so far in this book. I shouldn't call ladies "girls" or "gals." I shouldn't have hired only women to work the floor. I should call them "servers" instead of "waitresses." and I certainly shouldn't have insisted they wear sexually provocative costumes. But that was then and this is now. Sorry, ladies.

Speaking of personnel, I recall a meeting in San Francisco where a stock analyst was discussing equal opportunities for employees. He asked me, "Is your company broken down by sex?" I told him, "That's not our problem ... alcohol maybe, but not sex." After some strange looks, I thought I'd better get back to business and told them the numbers they were looking for: approximately fifty-five to forty-five ratio, women employees being the higher number of the two.

Anyway, I was talking about show business, wasn't I?

So now it's time to open the doors. Someone switches from harsh spots and fluorescents to more subtle mood lighting, replaces rock 'n' roll with background music and ta da ... they're ready.

The manager can finally say "Let's go to work," the curtain

rises and the door is opened to you, the customers.

During the next several hours, hundreds of people will come and go at a Stuart Anderson's. The tempo escalates. The atmosphere comes alive. The hum of the voices blends with the music, steamy smoke from steak platters drifts upward, tantalizing odors waft from passing trays – all these and more become part of the atmosphere.

The employees are now all professional, smiling at the customers to be sure but the interplay between them is altered because now their focus has shifted to helping each other make the public happy.

The point is, in the restaurant business, the employees have to depend on each other. If any one person misses his or her cue for whatever reason, the well-oiled machinery of teamwork will slowly grind to a halt. It doesn't matter if it's the dishwasher, cashier, hostess, bartender, cook or busser; they must pull together and give unasked for assistance when needed.

If the dishwasher quits doing his job, there'll be no clean plates; if the bus persons slow down, there'll be no clean tables at which to eat; if the servers quit, the food won't get to the tables hot, garnished or otherwise.

Consider a really good conductor: he probably isn't a master of each instrument individually but he knows how they should sound together.

You get the picture.

I had many faithful and dedicated restaurant employees. Most of my key management personnel, as well as many of the restaurant employees, stayed with me until my retirement. Some are still with the company.

It was one of the most important parts of my success: selecting the right person for the right job.

I only wish this concept worked as well on a ranch. But if I sent one of the hands out to the North Forty to mend fences and he goofed off and took a little nap, so what? It wouldn't directly affect the other hands. There was certainly no way he could bring a halt to the entire operation.

For some maddening reason, I just couldn't get or keep decent ranch help. If they were really good, I guess they successfully operated their own spread and didn't feel they had to work for someone else. In retrospect, I may have asked too much of them. It's hard to say.

After the lunch crowd, everything begins to slow, the short-term workers leave and the full-time help relaxes until the curtain rises again for the evening performance. Now there are two shows: one in the dining room and one in the lounge. If the customers leave happy, it means they liked the show and when you ask them why, you'll probably hear about the food and/or the service. They don't always realize the part the atmosphere played in creating their overall satisfaction.

Lots of times after leaving an eatery, I would ask my dining partner to describe the carpet, ceiling, music, tablecloths or what the servers were wearing. I usually heard amazingly few details because every little thing contributes to the aura of a space, whether home, office, or restaurant. Try this on your friends or spouse.

It is our duty and obligation as restaurateurs to provide for our customers' comfort and, in turn, for our own profit.

What is this thing called atmosphere?

It's nebulous; as hard to define as
it is to create. However, if you don't succeed in setting an appropriate mood,
you'll have to operate entirely
on the quality of food and pricing. In such
a competitive business, that might not be
enough. You need every edge you can get.

Some of what made the *Black Angus* restaurants unique in the beginning evolved quite by accident. One day I went to Del Teet Furniture in Seattle to have lunch with my friend and some-time-investor, Bill Teeter, who you met earlier.

While waiting, I glanced around the store and noticed he had separated his room displays with sheets of clear, smoky plastic. I asked him if he thought we could separate our booths and tables with this see-through Plexiglas material. Customers would be able to see the whole space while maintaining privacy and cigarette smoke would go up to the ventilators instead of into a neighbor's face. Bill thought it was a great idea, and this feature became a standard throughout the chain.

This little amenity was much appreciated, especially by the power-lunch bunch and those involved in the kinds of intimate affairs that have always been a part of the restaurant business. In using these dividers, we created a unique look that felt right even though the material brought with it special cleaning problems caused by static electricity.

My friend Bill was quite the innovator and came through in other ways. He helped me experiment with various table heights, sizes, and coverings (plasticized wood tops with logo insets, that sort of thing) and with table lighting. We tried candles but dripping was a problem as was the possibility of fire and accident hazards, which insurance companies frown upon. It's a known fact that women prefer candlelight and men like to see what they're eating, so we compromised. We put a little more light on the table with a Scandinavian wooden fixture that hung not so low that it hid your partner but not so high you had to stare at the bulb. Unknowingly, we had established another Black Angus signature.

Other than the actual ranch photos and real Washington State-registered brands, the Black Angus Restaurants never had paraphernalia such as horseshoes, ropes, stirrups, or a saddle in its stage setting as long as I was involved. Nothing against those items, they just seemed too ordinary.

We did use something from the ranch, though: real barn wood bleached from the sun, spattered with moss, square nails sticking out and lots of knotholes. I had a number of old falling-down barns and some of my neighbors didn't mind us cleaning up their junk barns, at least for a while. Soon enough they realized there was value there and the free-loading was over.

When my expansion took hold, we ran out of real barn wood, so we created a product that looked old by using acid. Not bad, but not great either. In any event, it worked and I abandoned my search for decorating treasures ... my lovely old barn wood. I miss the hunt.

> **TIP:** Many restaurants achieve early
> success with gimmicks. But for the long,
> successful run you need to perfect the quality of
> your food and the efficiency of your service.
> Interest driven by gimmicks dies out fast; think of
> them like starters on an engine.

Who's the most important person?

Another activity that took place before the curtain went up was the regular employee meeting. Fun? For me, yes. Actually, I felt you could never learn anything worthwhile at a meeting unless the leader or moderator shut up, listened, and limited the time.

Despite this opinion, the day before we opened a restaurant, we got together with all new employees. I always had a ball with the group, kidding and teasing, even while hoping to make a serious point or two. Approximately one hundred new people were included in a launch, mostly young and mostly nervous.

Without introducing myself, I'd start in. "Who's the most important person in the restaurant?" I'd ask, pointing to a young guy or gal for an answer. The response was usually a nervous: "You are!"

"And who am I?"

"You're the owner, with his name all over the place."

"That might be, but you're wrong about the most important person. It's not me. Try again."

"My new manager?" someone yelled.

"Nope!" I answered. "So who is it?"

From somewhere the correct response would finally come back: "THE CUSTOMER!" (I believe they got a whole lot of help from the trainers.)

"Right." I would give the person a compliment for helping out and tell him or her that I knew they'd do great in their work.

During this session, we'd also emphasize that, while the customer is most important, he or she is not necessarily "always right." That old catch phrase is too broad a statement for my taste. Important, yes, always right, not necessarily. There are times you have to back up your employee because there are some real jerks out there.

I would go on to tell them: "About three out of every four people you see here will make it, so if you try really hard tomorrow, it'll be worth the effort. Look around you. Some of the people here will become your very good friends. Please remember that employees are not allowed to date while working at the same restaurant." (This is like trying to keep the tide from rushing in to the shore.)

"Now, take a minute and say hello to the people around you." When everyone had settled back down, I'd continue: "Now, I'd like to give this microphone to someone here and have them tell us who they are." I'd move through the group.

"Why is everyone looking the other way? It's okay if you felt a moment of fear. That's natural. My point is, it should be the last time you feel fear in this restaurant. We do not operate by fear. It's not the atmosphere we want or will allow.

"We will pay you for the hours you punch on the time clock but we have to earn the extra effort you put into those hours.

"And we have a saying for all you food servers: 'The last three feet is where it happens.' Remember, the future of this restaurant depends on what happens in that space."

> **TIP:** Good service can save a bad meal
> but a good meal can't save bad service.

I end with, "You'll be encouraged to take part in the monthly meetings and be part of this family. There are some rules and no-no-s and I'll let your manager run through those. And here he is . . ."

> **TIP:** Always give the no-no-s
> and boring things to someone else.

Does it sound like I scram when the nitty-gritty of the meeting starts? You're right! It's one of the perks of being the founder. However, when it came to the vice presidents and directors, if any discipline was needed, it was by your truly. This brings back the memory of one incident and my great ability to do same.

I always gave lots of rein to my key people, many of whom had to travel widely. How much and where to were decisions I usually let them make. The "leader of our bands," Bob Anderson (no relation, but a good friend), was our entertainment director and was in charge of placing live groups or deejays in our lounges. With close to a hundred locations spread over the western United States, this was a demanding position and commanded a hefty part of our budget.

I remember one time when an IRS agent was looking at

our books. He noticed the entertainment account and exclaimed, "Oh my, this is big. You people must really have a good time." We changed the name of that account in a hurry!

IN MY OFFICE, <u>NOW!</u>

Bob was in a little trouble with me. Because he reported to me directly, this particular violation was mine to handle. Bob was young, tall, blond, handsome, single, and had a great wit, a dangerous combination.

I'm not prone to giving anyone a bad time, so to get in the proper mood I spent the morning recalling all the bad things that had ever happened to me: divorces and the price of same; misadventures in the stock market ... especially the commodities; loans to "friends" who never paid me back. When I was thinking mean enough, I called Bob and said, "Into my office, now!"

What I wasn't prepared for was his new hair-do. He had gone out and got a curly permanent, which in all fairness, was the cool thing to do at that time. When I saw this silly-looking head full of frizzy, baby curls, I knew I was in trouble. He looked like he'd stuck his finger in a light socket.

As I started to lose it, I peered down at my desk and told him I'd have to red flag his personnel record. My mouth tightened and it sounded like someone else talking. Looking up at Bob, all I could see were the kinky curls and I just couldn't keep my mean mood. I tried hard to maintain control and stop the desk from shaking. You know that feeling when somebody farts in church and you fight to keep from breaking up? That's exactly what was happening to me.

How are you going to stay tough when you're right on the edge of losing it? I told him to go away and come back another day. Lucky for him, he was leaving on a road trip. So I took one last glance at the back of his head and totally broke up.

You can imagine what this did to my tough image!

I guess I wasn't the only one who reacted this way because, a couple of days later, he had his hair straightened.

Now, without warning, it's test time!

Periodically I would meet with the vice presidents, directors, as well as the district and store managers. One of my nicer nicknames was "The Quiz Master" because of the written tests I gave. Since I liked to look smart, I knew all the answers.

In the first section I asked approximately 50 specific questions about their store or district, such as:

Part One: Costs & Percentages

1. What's your laundry cost?
Cost $_____   % of Gross _____

2. What's your bar labor cost?
Cost $_____   % of Gross _____

3. What's your current food cost?
Cost $_____   % of Gross _____

4. What's your highest selling lunch special?
Cost $_____   % of Gross _____

Obviously, I don't expect you to answer the above questions, but you might like to try the next set.

Remember, this is the restaurant business. (The answers are at the end of the chapter.)

Part Two: Management Style

1. What do we consider the most important ability for a manager:

a. Communications upward
b. Communications downward
c. Sociability
d. Ability to delegate

2. In seeking to create customer satisfaction, the most vital thing to remember is:
a. We must promptly adjust all customer complaints
b. We must know what the customer wants
c. Employees create the customer satisfaction
d. We must have a good chef

3. The best treatment for grapevine rumors is to:
a. Ignore them
b. Find out who starts them
c. Combat them with the truth
d. Fire the rumor mongers

4. If a restaurant is losing volume and money, the first thing the manager should do is:
a. Analyze costs
b. Study employee performance
c. Study his own performance
d. Make a chart and see his banker

5. The most basic thing to remember in employee discipline is:
a. Don't put it off
b. Allow a cooling-off period
c. Get all the facts
d. Make an example of the case

In the third and last section I finished with my "killer quiz," and if they got the answers in advance, all the better. You'll see what I mean.

"All right, everybody, write down as many of your employees names as you can, both first and last. Next, write the spouses' names and then, if you can, how many children they have. Good luck!"

There were never any 100-percent winners, but you must remember there were 70 to 80 full- or part-timers in each restaurant.

It was no surprise to me that the managers with the highest percentages on this section usually had the highest morale. Even if any one of them wanted to cheat by writing the answers down on their cuff for next time, it served its purpose.

There was one person who could get really close to 100 percent – Rich Chorich, who is still a friend. He could and still can give me employee names, the dates when restaurants opened, who managed them and the list goes on. He's an avid sports fan and can also supply you with a degree of trivia that is unbelievable.

Before seriously considering the above multiple choices, I want to give a dissertation on the Stuart Anderson School of Restaurant Management.

Some textbooks, some of the suits at Saga and, maybe some of the readers might take exception to my philosophy of hiring, training, and motivating but my views are strongly held. I don't believe a person can learn charm, personality, or attitude. If you dig deep enough, you'll find these assets in your interviewing.

I have always sought those who would become a member of a family atmosphere. (More on this important point later.) Motivation is ongoing and accomplished by treating all employees with great respect and appreciation for the many things they do. Have you hugged your servers lately?

One thing to remember: Most of our new employees are young adults (eighteen to twenty-six) who are not looking for long-term, career opportunities. They simply want to earn money for school or increase the family income in the early years of marriage.

Labor turnover is a given in the restaurant business. However, the Stuart Anderson Chain had one of the lowest rates in the hospitality industry. And to those who stayed with us a long time, may the sun continue to shine warmly on their faces.

Now, I know you can answer the above multiple-choice questions. Try them again.

Note: All the correct answers are (c).

Chapter 9

Give me your Coat and Drop your Pants!

They were a great source of income and at the same time a source of irritation. From this chapter title, you probably know what I'm talking about – restaurant coatrooms. It was years ago that we eliminated them from our design because, despite the additional income from tips, they were a pain in the ass for both the operator and the customer.

In colder climates, the tips were substantial and all we had to do was babysit their coats for an hour or two. As operators, we hated the practice because of the frequent loss or exchange of a coat or hat. The quickest way to lose a customer was to give him or her the wrong garment (unless it was nicer than the one checked but somehow this NEVER happened).

Lawsuits were threatened, we purchased new hats and coats and then insurance companies started dropping us like hot potatoes. It was the custom to split the tips between the coatroom attendant and the restaurant. If some sharp gal paid a flat fee for the concession you can imagine how involved it could get determining half the tips or what the concession was worth. Cash flow varied greatly with the number of customers and the weather.

I once offered an up-and-coming manager the income from the coatroom in addition to his regular pay to encourage him to move to a store way out in the cold boondocks.

Years later he would confide how profitable those days

had been. I won't mention his name because I don't know whether the IRS got their full share.

The coatrooms were not manned at all times. In the late afternoon, the counter remained open and we would hang a sign saying, "Not Responsible for Lost Articles." Whoa! That sign did not mean squat. They were either going to sue or never come back.

We had an unusually large loss of articles at one particular store, day and night. Somebody was making a living ripping us off. None of the employees had a view of the front door or the coatroom so I contacted a friend and well-known private eye, Ward Keller, who came up with an idea of rigging a coat hanger. When you took the weight off the arms of this hanger, it triggered an almost invisible wire drilled through the wall, which led to a red bulb set up in the bar. I used my own cashmere coat as bait. It was handsome, light tan, and fairly new and we knew it would be the first one picked.

Ward and I ordered a couple of martinis and all we could do was stare at that dumb bulb. A big snore! We were cut out of the loop with the others in the bar and felt more than a little ridiculous. Of course, we hadn't mentioned our caper to anyone.

After two drinks, we decided to call one of Ward's operatives to take over and we went out to look for something more exciting to do. When we returned a few hours later, we looked into the coatroom. The coat was gone, the hanger bars had been sprung and my first thought was, "Oh good, we've got the S.O.B. and now we can end these losses." We couldn't wait to get into the bar and find out who they'd caught. Was it a regular customer or someone I knew? I couldn't wait to get my hands on this guy for all the grief he'd caused us.

We walked into the bar. The light was on and the operative was sitting in a booth slurring words and trying to charm a couple of lookers. He wasn't quite sure where he was but he was having quite a lively time, having totally forgotten why he was there in the first place. All this work we did to build and disguise the trap was in vain. We never did catch the person and I never saw my coat again. Oh, the agony of defeat!

The good news was that Ward never sent me a bill. He did give me a ride in his private plane and flew me all over the Seattle area. Big deal - I would rather have had my coat back.

Another coatroom in another store almost ruined Christmas. One Christmas Eve afternoon, three of us decided we had better go shopping for our wives. We were at that stage in our marriages where we felt like going to the equivalent of Frederick's of Hollywood or Victoria's Secret. All of us spent an embarrassing hour and finished our duty with three or more beautifully wrapped flimsies and headed back to the bar. I took my presents to my office, Bob took his with him to the bar and Ed put his in the coatroom.

The bar was jumping as usual on Christmas Eve day and after a quick drink we started to head for home when Ed let out a yelp. His presents had gone missing from the unattended coatroom and he looked like he was about to cry. Too late now; all the stores were closed. Bob and I decided the only civilized thing we could do was to each donate one of our gift boxes to the cause. The only problem was we forgot our wives weren't the same sizes and the personal notes had been placed inside. We were all now short on gifts and it didn't make for a perfect Christmas for any of us.

On a different Christmas Eve in that same cloakroom, our fruit and produce vendor had left two beautiful fruit baskets. One basket had a tag reading "To Stu" and the other "To Bruce," my senior vice president. I quickly moved mine to the office and I notified Bruce Attebery that his was waiting in the cloakroom.

A short while later, my attorney, Dick Dameyer, dropped by and gave me an unexpected Christmas gift. (Maybe all those hefty legal fees had created some guilt!) I deftly removed my name from the basket and presented it to him as his gift from me. Sure!

About a week later, Bruce showed me a card he'd discovered at the bottom of his basket. It said, "Bruce, we hope you enjoyed the fruit and thank you for the business over the years." My, oh, my, did I blow that one! I waited for the repercussions, but they never came.

I finally had to ask Dick about it. He never saw the card

in his basket. He'd presented the gift I'd given him, with the addition of his own card, to the late Senator Henry Jackson.

I could just hear the Senator saying, "Who the hell is Stu?"

The hell with coatrooms ... hats aren't worn much anymore and expensive furs aren't as popular. If the truth be known, I really don't care what the guy who comes in from the cold does! It's not my problem anymore.

DOOR NO. 1, 2, OR 3?

Behind the scenes of the restaurants you patronize are some additional doors. Which do you choose: 1, 2, or 3?

One thing for sure, those names they use are dumb and dumber:

      a. Bucks or Does
      b. Braves or Squaws
      c. His or Hers
      d. Sheilas or Blokes
      e. Buoys or Gulls
      f. Pointers or Setters
      g. Birdies or Bogies
      h. Cocks or Hens

Then there are the cartoons or cute plaques of various males and females dressed in odd clothes on the door. Do you always know which door is which? We're not talking brain surgery here, but you have to admit, some operators ought to be horsewhipped.

When I remodeled my first restaurant at the Caledonia Hotel, the men's room had splashed across the mirror: "Here's where Anderson ran out of money."

It was true; I figured I couldn't make any money in there anyway. Can you see the handwriting on the wall? Then you've visited my first "john."

I once asked a favorite couple of mine how they met and he said he got her phone number off our men's room wall.

She didn't take kindly to him telling us this story.

What is it that happens to guys when they get into a public restroom? They seem to go bananas with the old pen or pencil; "boink" this and that – then they tear the toilet-paper holder off the wall. I hate to tell you this, but in some areas, women provide graffiti too and it isn't pretty.

Frankly, it's a good thing women don't get to see the things said on men's restroom walls and vice versa.

If you've had a chance to visit the john in any rest stop along the interstate in this great country, you know they're built like the inside of a tank. We didn't have to go to that extreme but close to it. We tried to make it look classy by tiling everything we could with the upshot that tiles are hard to write on. It was expensive but a whole lot better than hanging the daily sports page over the urinals or installing a chalk board that puffed chalk dust everywhere. They even scribbled stupid words on the signs we placed on the wall, which said, "All employees must wash their hands before returning to work."

Just as an aside ... I really got a chuckle out of the Jerry Seinfeld TV program where the chef joins Jerry in the men's room, does his duty, and then tells Jerry he's going to fix him his special as he walks out without washing his hands. There goes the old appetite! As Julia Child said on nouvelle cuisine, "It's so beautifully arranged on the plate, you know someone's fingers have been all over it."

While tiling restrooms is not required by local ordinances, the proper number of plumbing fixtures is. Often local ordinances require you to do something stupid but you have to do it or you're toast.

The women's john, for example, should have twice as many fixtures as the men's. But they never require that. How many times have we seen women standing outside waiting to get in?

One of my all-time favorite bathroom stories involves a letter I got from a lady I didn't know. The gist of the letter read as follows:

"Dear Stuart,
"Thank you, thank you, thank you! Thank you for my new sofa, new coffee table, new lamps, and new carpet."

(My wife opened the letter and was pretty nervous after the first few sentences, wondering what I'd been up to.)

The letter went on, *"Let me explain. My husband went to sit down on the toilet in your restaurant, and because the seat was broken, he fell sideways and injured himself. All of the above items were purchased from the settlement we received from your corporation ...."*

That story reminds me of my good friend, Linda Harrison, who claims that every man is born with a book that tells them how to behave and do the "right thing" with the opposite sex. Some examples for all you women out there:

Just so you know there's a legitimate reason, Rule #5 in the Male Manual warns men NOT to put the toilet seat down when finished. Rule #3 tells them not to ask directions no matter how lost they are. Why do you think Moses wandered around the desert for 40 years?

Rule #16 forbids them to pick up their socks and put them in the dirty-clothes hamper. Men must leave their clothes where they fall when removed.

Rule #2 gives men full control of the TV remote. Women may be allowed to use it but only if there's nothing the male wants to watch.

Rule #14 teaches men to be able to do absolutely NOTHING. This one especially drives women crazy.

Rule #15 encourages patience. If a man needs something but there's no one around, he has only to be patient and someone will come through the room to get whatever it is he desires. No need to get up from his comfortable position, no matter what.

There's a lot more but you get the idea.

Have you about had it with bodily functions and the rooms built for same? I hear you. One more experience and we'll mosey.

There's a fascinating men's room in a club in California but I'd best not tell you specifically where because you'll go there for all the wrong reasons.

After dinner one night, I went to the john and when I stepped up to the urinal, a light beam was triggered which revealed a beautiful, life-sized, scantily-clad, woman on the wall smack in front of me. She was peering down at what I had pulled out, commenting on what a dandy I had. Some video! I was so embarrassed; there was no way anything was going to happen after that. I tried the next stall and the same thing happened. It was just a little much.

One of the problems restaurateurs face is the unexpected visits by the Health Department. This can lead to a lot of grief, possible shut downs or even losing you're A-1 rating.

My Vice President Bruce Attebery and I had the idea one day to hire a good gal to work for us and train her by having her accompany the Health Department during inspections so she could figure out what they were looking for. The managers nick-named her Susie Spotless or Gloria Glitter and it was one of the better ideas we had because it took away the worry of inspections. She learned it all and did her job well.

After hiring her, food was kept at the right temperature and was dated and rotated so it stayed fresh. Cleaning supplies had to be separated from food storage and hand-washing stations installed where needed. You couldn't have any thumbtacks above food prep areas. She made sure the bathrooms, kitchen, and the interior including the walls, were spotless. She even checked the exterior areas.

This became our system and it gave us a lot of comfort. However, instead of the Health Department, the managers now had the fear of an unexpected visit from Susie Spotless. They said she was tougher on them than any county worker. But this procedure made them perform the way they should.

I figure I've spent millions of dollars on johns over the years, so I know of what I speak. I'll bet you can guess where I spent most of our money on our newly remodeled homes. Right! I had a bathroom to die for in the last house: steam shower with a foot Jacuzzi; TV with remote; lots of books; thick wall-to-wall carpet; a sky-lighted cathedral ceiling; wonderful art; and yes, even some beautiful tile.

Our current home in the Desert also has a steam shower, granite and everything else I deserve! I call my room "Door No. 3," and there better not be anyone writing on the wall.

Chapter 10

The Chef's Way or the Highway

The restaurant business fit me to a tee. It would let me sleep late even though it's a career that carries with it some of the longest hours of any profession a person can choose. My normal "shifts" were from ten a.m. to eight or nine p.m., six days a week.

One day, my body got confused with ranch life where I rose with the sun and I ended up at the restaurant early to look at the books. Someone from the kitchen crew let me in. I realized I didn't have a key to the office so thought I would just sit by the window in the banquet room and wait until the bookkeeper came in. No one would know I was there because it wasn't part of the daily activity so I had time to experience something rather spellbinding.

The banquet room overlooked the parking lot of the Number One Black Angus and faced toward the service door. I noticed a lot of delivery trucks moving around, a sight I expected to see. But the other people I saw arriving threw me. They showed up in scruffy clothes appearing as though they hadn't been home for a while. Some wore bandannas while others resembled flashers with bare legs sticking out from under their coats. They would knock and be admitted, this sorry-looking bunch. I didn't know who they were at first and then it dawned on me that they had to be my beautiful employees.

Do you ever meet people who are out of their normal place and dress, like a clerk in a store you frequent or a nurse from your doctor's office? You know them but can't figure out why. It was interesting to watch.

Then here came a service truck from our meat company. The uniformed driver, who looked young and pleasant, had a loaded cart that he rolled to the kitchen. He went back to his truck, came out with his cart, went to a car, opened the trunk, put a good-sized package in there and then went back to the kitchen. I recognized the chef's car right away and wondered what the hell was going on. Since it appeared that something we paid for was going home instead of to the walk-in refrigerator, I wanted to take a look right away.

I'll bet you think I should have canned him immediately and you're probably right. I decided to go to the chef and say, "I want to go to your car and see what's in the trunk. Let me have the key."

Then I started thinking about it and what a fabulous job he had been doing on the day shift. He was pleasant, prepared great lunch food, kept a clean kitchen and had a happy crew. He had everything working just right and was everything I looked for in a good chef.

So I thought of other possibilities. Maybe he'd paid for it. Maybe it was nothing crooked. I decided to just think about it for a spell. For one thing, he had a personality with a big ego that would probably cause him to stomp off if I accused him.

I could see we were prepping for a large mid-day crowd so I came up with this great idea to let the situation ride and then call a meeting that afternoon and talk about honesty and thievery and what it can do to a business.

I included the entire crew and told them their job could be in jeopardy. I was trying not to look at the chef but I must have looked at him at least ten times. He didn't act guilty. I spoke fondly about the old days when we used to have a lot of light fingers in the Ringside Room because, prior to credit cards, everything was paid for with cash.

For example, the drinks in those days were mostly "waterback" which meant a glass for the liquor and a glass of water on the side. So we lined up shot glasses and poured the booze into them and people paid cash as we went along. it was obviously very tempting for the bartender to pocket some of that.

(Yes, you younger people, I started way back before credit cards. And when those companies did come in, they charged like 8% which was extremely steep. Today it varies between 1.5 to 2.5 percent.)

TIP: Point-of-sales systems today help a lot in controlling both restaurant and bar sales so it pays to invest in a good one. Watch out if servers have a lot of voids. In the bar, keep the liquor room locked. After removing a bottle, have the bartender put the empty in the carton and sign out for the new bottle.

Keep tips in a separate jar, not the till. Never allow big bags behind the bar. This will discourage bringing a bottle from home, selling it and pocketing the money. Don't allow bartender/server relationships. A good bookkeeper can pick up on a lot of trends if they're not fitting the norm.

Anyhow, I brought all this up so the employees knew that I was sincere about it. I promised them they could report it to me and I would keep their name out of it. Or, in some cases, they could warn the thief to stop. I emphasized that we'd all be losers if the business failed due to thievery as every ones' jobs would go down the toilet with it. I hoped this would be the solution.

For the record, no one reported anything.

At first I agonized about this and continued to wonder what was in that chef's car going down the highway. Eventually I decided that my decision was a mistake. I should have listened to that small voice in my head, got the manager and had the chef accompany us to see what was in that trunk.

Soon after, that chef left the company for another restaurant and I lost track of him.

Theft should never be tolerated even though it can be part of the business. With great management you can practically eliminate it.

TIP: **The best prevention
is to thoroughly check
prospective employees' backgrounds
before you hire.**

One good practice came from this experience: we had one of our bussers guard the back door and monitor everything that came in and went out. When idle, he wrapped silverware in the napkins, filled salt and peppers or saw to various other similar jobs. A surveillance camera at the back door is also a good move.

TIP: **A good honest person
takes exception to you having suspicions
about his actions so take great care who you
accuse of wrong doing.**

When Bad Things happen to Good People

The restaurant business has always been very much a cash business. Although businessmen out there envy us because of that, there are disadvantages. Almost every employee on the floor handles cash, which allows theft to raise its ugly head. But how much of it ends up where it doesn't belong is less than most people think.

I'm not proud about what I'm going to tell you now, but years ago, we hired a surveillance service to spy on our people, who were informed this was our practice when we hired them. A report would come back with a name, what store, time of day, etc. The spy would continue on and on writing about what he experienced.

What did it tell us? That basically this practice was a waste of a man's time and our liquor. Reading the reports gave me an uncomfortable feeling of Big Brother and we soon stopped doing it, chalking the experience up as an expensive lesson. The spy had cost me more than I was losing.

The best control I found was to interview and hire with care and then treat all the people with respect. The vast majority of restaurant employees are honest and don't want to work in an atmosphere where light fingers are operating. In fact, they usually report problems like these and become your theft control. Pretty nifty, huh?

TIP: **It's better to be occasionally cheated than perpetually suspicious.**

Theft from the outside was a much bigger headache. We worked to prevent this by using bigger and better safes, installing heavier doors with peepholes, surveillance cameras and training the employees. But even with all the right procedures in place, there were vulnerable moments of exposure: when the safes were opened; when deposits were made; and of course, trips to the bank.

There was one case where our attempted solution to the problem bit us in the butt. My bookkeeper was nervous about depositing the receipts especially with large amounts of cash involved. So I delegated this job to a "gofer" – a big guy who worked for us for more than a year. He took the deposits by a different route every time.

One day the route took this overweight fart away forever. Unfortunately, it was a big weekend deposit and we were self-insured, which meant there wasn't an insurance company to collect from. Even after fifty years I find myself looking for that thief, but that train left the station long ago.

Another time we got burned even worse. Following another big weekend at our Spokane store, the assistant cook was the first employee to arrive that Monday morning. He was confronted in the kitchen by three gunmen who demanded he open the safe but the poor man didn't know how. The gunmen then put him in the large, refrigerated walk-in, and as others arrived, they, too, were escorted to the walk-in, which was kept at thirty-eight degrees.

Since it was summertime and short-sleeved shirt weather, you can imagine how these eight or nine early arrivals had suffered.

About 9:30 a.m., our bookkeeper arrived. She emphatically told the gunmen she didn't have the combination, so into the walk-in she went to face the others, who were freezing in their light clothing. They also knew damn well she had the combination and quickly convinced her to tell.

I appreciated her loyalty and courage but the company's instruction has always been never to take risks like that because a human life is much more valuable than any amount of money.

The three gunmen were apprehended but served no time on some technicality. That subject warrants a whole other book.

We are left armed with nothing but our tears.

Chapter 11

John Wayne, Hogs, Horses & Hot Women

The article on the next page appeared in
the *Press Enterprise* (See boxed paragraph.)

This article was faulty in more than a few ways. I think I know how the story got started, which brings to mind another big moment I'll never forget – when John Wayne "dropped in." It happened at an RV park in Baja, Mexico a long time ago when I had a camper. I think it was around 1972 and I was with Dick Dameyer, my attorney and friend. We were on our way to Cabo San Lucas to visit a contractor buddy and thought to mix business with some of the finest marlin fishing in the world. Although we always practiced catch-and-release, the battle was exhilarating.

John Wayne heard that I ran around in a fun camper I'd named the "Bill Teeter Designed Camper." We even had a telephone that looked real but didn't work as it was way before cell phones.

(Once we were at a stop sign and someone handed the phone to the guy in the pickup next to us and said, "It's for you." The guy took it with a stunned look on his face, the light changed and he drove off with our telephone!)

Meanwhile, back at the story ... John Wayne came knocking with a bang, bang, bang that shook the whole RV. I opened the door and experienced that weird moment when you think you recognize someone but can't believe it's who you think it is.

Next to the house is the huge pool that John Wayne built. "The Duke" owned the ranch from about 1938 to 1949. He and his partner, Stuart Anderson of steak house fame, raised hogs at Rancho Pavor eal, and cattle at their Red River Ranch in Arizona.

▶ A 6,000-acre bed-and-breakfast ranch gives city slickers a chance to ride into the past without leaving too many creature comforts behind.

By Gordon Johnson
The Press-Enterprise

SAGE

The trail snaked around clumps of white sage, thorny cactus and yucca stalks crowned with yellow blooms, squeezing the motley band of riders into single file.

Just ahead, a woman in crisp Wranglers moved nicely with the paddle-footed, parade gait of her Peruvian Paso horse.

Then, without warning, she grabbed her hat by its brim, leaned sharply to the left and waved it at a small lizard on the trail, trying to shoo it from advancing horse hooves.

"You better get moving, little fellow," she said in a voice sweet enough to calm a child after a nightmare.

Surely, this was a first. A cowhand worried about a lizard on the trail?

But then, city slickers are like that.

They had come — a half dozen of them — from the wilds of Simi Valley and Mission Viejo and San Pedro to work cattle on Rancho Pavoreal, a 6,000-acre bed-and-breakfast ranch east of Temecula and south of Hemet, where dudes eat dust by day and filet mignon by night.

They had come to get a taste of the Old West, but a comfortable taste. They had come to the right place.

The ranch's main house is long and low with a front porch that runs the length of it. Big picture windows overlook the brushy valley where cattle and coyotes roam. In the distance, Mt. Palomar rises to meet the clouds, with its white-domed observatory sticking out like a fly on a birthday cake.

Pavoreal means peacock in Spanish, but there isn't a peacock in sight. Instead, white geese waddle the grounds, greeting visitors with indignant honks. When not guarding the place, they feed in the large pond below the house along with ducks, bullfrogs and mosquito fish.

Next to the house is the huge pool that John Wayne built. "The Duke" owned the ranch from about 1938 to 1949. He and his partner, Stuart Anderson of steak house fame, raised hogs at Rancho Pavoreal, and cattle at their Red River Ranch in Arizona.

But more than a livestock ranch,

it was a getaway lodge where Wayne's buddies like Andy Devine, Gabby Hayes and Gene Autry would fly in for a few days of pleasure riding and lounging around the pool.

Allen and Joanne Senall took over the ranch in 1989 after it had been abandoned for more than 20 years. Hippies and other transients had wrecked the house, but a year and a half of hard work restored it to its former glory.

Now Allen runs the ranch and Joanne takes care of the bed-and-breakfast end of the operation.

Please see RANCH, C-4

This was exciting! He asked if he and this other fellow would be welcome to take a look. I replied, "Sure, come on in."

Do you think I would have said no?

The Duke, as most knew him, was interested in the design Bill had come up with. Since he spent a lot of time in his movie trailer, he thought he might pick up some new ideas to make it more like home. His friend took pictures while we talked.

Well, we ended up having a few drinks and we both could hold our liquor in those days. Then he called me the hog farmer. I replied "I'll raise pigs when pigs fly!" Well, he kept teasing me about it so, to get even, I informed him I was a real cattle rancher and he was a fake cowboy. I got ready to duck but I guess the drinks we'd guzzled had mellowed him and he just laughed.

It turned out we'd both went to USC. At the same time, you ask? No, give me a break; he was a good 15 years older. But we did talk about that good old school and how we missed our time there.

John was born in Iowa and since I had worked there for a couple of years, we also had that in common. On the way in, he must have spoken to someone in the RV park because somehow he knew I was "The Steak Man." That was a lot better than being called Mr. Pig.

He was a great guy, very down to earth and fun to be around. I asked if I could call him "Big John" and he said I could. He laughed a lot, which surprised me, because he always seemed quite serious in his movies. I asked him to teach me his walk which also made him laugh. I never managed to master that rolling gait but if I had and then showed up at one of my restaurants sauntering like John, I'm sure they would have opened the back door and let me just keep walking on out.

Big John wanted to talk about ranching and I wanted to talk about his movies and the women he worked with like Maureen O'Hara. He said he wasn't crazy about riding horses and I informed him my Hondas were my horses. Horses were too much trouble. You had to catch them, put on all their gear, get on and off to open gates or move irrigation equipment, water and feed them and the list goes on.

I could jump on my Honda 3-wheeler, turn the key and I was off and running. I could tow a wagon with needed supplies. I even designed a ramp that let me drive over the gates so I wouldn't need to open them. John said he had a spread in Arizona but admitted that, although he loved it, he wasn't much of a rancher. He said I was welcome to stop by sometime and give him some hints if I felt like it. Not sure if he was serious or not. I returned the invite, and he said he would plan on it next time he brought his boat up to the Seattle area. We could exchange ideas and whatnot.

I wonder if two half-cowboys make a whole one.

A publicity photo of John Wayne for the film *The Comancheros*, released by 20th Century Fox in 1961.

The article was not true because we never did a whit of business together. Maybe the Duke was teasing the author, Gordon Johnson, a well-known journalist and a good writer for the Press Enterprise, and was taken seriously by mistake.

I contacted Gordon recently but he had no recollection of who gave him that information. He's retired now and had no memory of how he'd connected the two of us. Whatever it was, Big John and I surely never raised hogs together.

Being half a cowboy, I loved John's movies. For a few years the Duke was the biggest money-maker in Hollywood. I think I've seen the vast majority of his films. Incidentally, if you get a chance, look for his movie, *The Searchers*. I felt it was his best although *Red River* would come in a close second.

I invited Big John to any one of our restaurants, which would have caused quite a stir. He made me promise I would not pre-announce his appearance as he was afraid he'd be swamped by fans and picture takers. If he just showed up, he could usually get his meal eaten before anyone figured it out. Sadly, he never made it. We had to settle for Charlton Heston instead – a pleasant surprise to the crew when he walked into one of the Black Angus Restaurants.

**TIP: Big John talked right wing politics
which was not the norm for Hollywood.
Like a good restaurateur, I agreed with him.
I always tried to go with the flow politically.**

**If I were with a republican or a democrat in the
restaurant I would politely nod to that person.
It's not too wise to get into politics publicly
because you're going to lose a lot of the
business from those on the other side.
I won't tell you where my heart is.**

Later on, the Duke and I visited about boats, a subject dear to my heart having been raised in Seattle. His converted Navy vessel, *Wild Goose,* was moored in the RV park where we were staying although he normally kept it in Newport Beach. After several hefty drinks, we parted company as he was heading north and I was heading south. I got up fairly early the next morning to go down and take a peek at his boat but they had already left. I was disappointed but he had said I could see it in Newport any time which reminds me of another fascinating story about how this connection led me to the boat I fell in love with – the awesome *Groote Beer.*

I wish I could have had more time with John but life busied up and we never did get together again. At the time, he said there was talk about him making another movie with Jimmy Stewart, which did happen. Can you name the two movies they were in together?

Big John passed away during his 72nd year on this earth after a battle with cancer. That's way too young.

Not many people know that John Wayne owned a big place in Arizona near Nogales, on the U.S./Mexico border. Called the *Red River Ranch,* The Duke bought it after he finished working on the film *Red River* there.

As I write this book, two sections of that spread are up for sale: the *26 Bar Ranch* at Eagar, Springerville, and *The Duke's Hill Ranch* near Nogales.

Chapter 12

The Days of Wine and Roses

By the time I'd opened 12 Black Angus Restaurants and was operating each as a separate entity, I was swamped with paperwork. The purpose of having that many corporations was to prevent one or two bad apples from dragging down the successful ones. Actually, all twelve were profitable and had positive cash flows, which I kept using for expansion. Even so, I was getting tired of the never ending meetings and financially, I was still hanging way out there in no-man's land.

The search for help from a "big daddy" had some options. Forget the banks; they got nervous every time they saw me coming. There was a remote chance to go public with a stock issue but I didn't have a long enough history of earnings. You know the old saying: "When you don't need the money, it's easy to get."

I decided to pursue a third option: finding a large company with cash reserves and arranging a compatible marriage. I traveled around the country with a merger specialist and found two likely candidates, one in the Midwest and one in the deep South.

I didn't seem to mesh well with one of the management groups and I didn't like the grim offices of the other (or their people who looked just as grim).

During my quest for the "Golden Grail," I ran into Saga Corporation which provided college, university, business and industry contracted feeding. They also had limited restaurant experience with Straw Hat Pizza and Velvet Turtle dinner houses.

I knew something about Velvet Turtle (VT) restaurants before I ran across Saga. In my travels researching new locations for Black Angus, I had become attached to one particular VT in the California market. I liked the display cooking featured in the lobby and the exterior and interior were tastefully done. At the time, I had no idea that we would become half-assed partners in the constant search for growth.

Wally Botello, the founder of the Velvet Turtle chain, was to become a good friend and I learned much at the feet of the "master," as I used to call him. Wally had panache in whatever he did. When I stayed with him at his Palm Springs townhouse, I was totally impressed by his interior design. My raves about his decor would eventually lead to a major gamble on my part.

Wally introduced me to the world-renowned interior designer Steven Chase of Palm Springs, Singapore, New York, and other exotic places. (At that time he was with Arthur Elrod and Associates.) Steve had decorated Wally's home and I decided I wanted him to do something for me. Steve and I became involved in my grand experiment in seafood. (That's right, seafood – but more on that later.)

I'm saddened to say Steve is gone now as is Wally, who went on to expand his five-store chain into twenty-one restaurants with Saga. Incidentally, twenty of the twenty-one Velvet Turtles are also long gone, but before Wally left us, he built and operated Wally's in Rancho Mirage, California. This is one of the renowned restaurants in the country and ably operated by his son, Michael.

The story of Wally's departure from Saga is a mystery to most of us who knew and worked with him. A new Velvet Turtle was opening in Texas and a liquor company had booked and paid for a banquet. The banquet was cancelled but the liquor people did not want a refund. So began the mystery: why would someone pay big bucks for a banquet and not use it?

Operating like Washington, D.C. lobbyists, liquor vendors used this unconventional maneuver to further their own interests. By paying some big bucks into VT's banquet account, they could influence the restaurant manager to purchase their line of liquor. This apparently was in violation of liquor control rules. The mystery is who knew what and when did they know it? I don't know if Wally was even aware of the transaction, but I do know he did not personally enrich himself. Yet he became Saga's scapegoat. He had to resign and so ended the saga of Wally, a man in command of his craft – building and managing restaurants. What a shame!

Yes, I'm getting ahead of myself, but Wally and his successful operation were a big part of the reason I made my first visit to Saga. I was impressed with the ambiance of the Velvet Turtles, investigated the ownership and so became aware of Saga Corporation.

One look at Saga headquarters and I was smitten. I don't know why that was so important to me, but it was. I called their location "The Campus." The site was in Menlo Park, California, overlooking the San Francisco Bay. The one- and two-story buildings were separated by large expanses of green. It was spectacular! I felt there had to be a pony in there somewhere.

People who could build such an office complex had to have a great enjoyment of beauty and feelings for the overall environment. I don't know who romanced whom, but the beginning negotiations went smoothly. My agent negotiated with their attorneys and they arrived at a stock-for-stock transaction as a tax-free exchange that worked well for both parties. Most importantly, I would continue to run the Black Angus Company.

I remember meeting the president of the restaurant group, Jim Morrell, who was also executive vice president of Saga. I think I've gotten that right, but who really cares – titles are boring anyway. Jim was a class act, and given that setting, I just wanted to know where to sign. Dorothy Parker describes "class" as "grace under pressure." Like any marriage, we had some pressure-packed times.

The merger for stock would take a few months, and before the final transfer, I was scheduled to meet the three founders, Bill Scandling, Harry "Hunk" Anderson, and Bill

Saga founders guarding the entrance to "the campus."
Left to right, Bill Scandling, Bill Laughlin and
Hunk Anderson. Photo courtesy of Bill Scandling.

Laughlin.

The three had met shortly after the conclusion of World War II when they were students at Hobart College in Geneva, New York. It was also there that they started a college feeding program because they were confident they could put out better food than what they were getting at Hobart. I was eager to meet them because I was amazed that three young guys could start such a business and remain equal in the power structure as it grew into a large corporation. I had heard they rotated the offices of chairman, president, and vice chairman without one wielding more power than the other two – surely an outstanding example of male bonding!

Jim Morrell's assistant, John Weaver, guided me around the campus to visit each founder's office. First I met Bill Scandling who appeared quite cool with his slicked-back hair, perfectly knotted tie and an office that reflected his dress and personality. It was one of those beautiful settings where you imagined if you moved too quickly, something might go horribly wrong. And when a person is dressed that neatly, it makes me feel like my zipper's at half-mast and there's a spot on my tie. I'm sure my pants were closed and my tie was clean but I had a long way to go.

As Bill appeared bored by the meeting, I thought the merger could be in trouble. But first impressions can be misleading and I should've known better. In the end, he was almost the savior of Saga. ALMOST!

Next in my little odyssey was Hunk Anderson who was married to a woman called "Moo." (I just HAD to meet someone with such an unusual name and when I did, it was a pleasure. She didn't at all fit the image I'd conjured up.) From the name Hunk, I imagined I'd be meeting a compatriot, a big fellow cowboy who might even have a little Swede in him. Outside of the butch haircut, Hunk didn't fit my image at all. He was neither large nor a cowboy. He had that look of "Who passed gas?" on his face. I later learned that expression disguised his intelligence.

Here again his office was spacious and full of stuff I eventually found out was modern art in the extreme. It looked like he was in the process of moving. I once asked him to attend our Western Experience Sale at the ranch where we sold registered cattle alternately with Western or American art. He peered at me as if I'd called him a dirty name and said, "Are you kidding? Western art? That's not art to me." That hurt.

He also appeared bored, but therein is my fascination with first impressions: they're not worth a damn!

Last of the three, but certainly not least, was Bill Laughlin, known as "Willy the Lock." Everything about this office was massive if you know what I mean ... a huge desk and furniture you sank way down into, all very intimidating.

Each office was totally different and all were quite large, as if keeping a balance among the founders. The man behind the desk appeared to be wearing his pajamas. In time I discovered he always wore loud, way-out clothing. No butch cut or slicked-back hair here; zippo! Next I noticed another large item, a huge dog lying in front of the desk. Being an old half cowboy, I love dogs and I always had a least two following me around the ranch. But I'd never seen a dog in an office on a business day. I felt like I might've been able to ride my horse into this interview.

As it turned out, Willy was not bored. He seemed fascinated by what he was saying. The marketing man of the group and a definite asset, he resembled other marketing types I'd known in that he could be one loose cannon. He was also a bit of a name dropper.

Once, while attending one of those frequent team-building sessions at some California resort, we broke for the day and moved out to the lawn. What captured our immediate attention was a tiger – I mean a huge, living, king-sized tiger – lying on the grass attached to a bitty pole with a way-too-small metal leash. We all approached with caution and circled the animal, even though his trainer was off to one side. What the hell was this all about? Go back to your jobs and be a tiger! Willy's idea. Anyone who thinks up things like that can't be all bad. I was impressed! It was an image no one was likely to forget.

All in all, the three founders had obviously accomplished much and created quite an organization. It was my feeling that since they were entrepreneurs and not MBAs, they'd allow me to run my business as I saw fit. They were contract feeders, which is almost the opposite of restaurant feeding. We all wanted happy customers but achieved our results from different directions.

I never worked closely with any of the three gentlemen, to my regret. We did mix socially once in a while but they were in Menlo Park and I was way off in Seattle. But since I was free to continue to run my corporation the way I wanted, that was just fine with me.

I believe they had a lot of confidence in Jim Morrell. He didn't know the restaurant business per se, but Jim was aware of his shortcomings, which was a good start. He was a quick study and an asset to management of both Black Angus and Saga.

Right after the formal signing of all the merger papers and the exchange of stock, John Weaver turned to me and said, "You are now a millionaire many times over." I replied, "I hear you, but it hasn't really sunk in yet. Guess I need a break in Hawaii for a few days."

While lying on the beach in Honolulu, I made over a million dollars.

Following the announcement in the Wall Street Journal, our stock moved up on the board. "Celebrate the moment of your life," as they say, but it was not meant to be. There isn't much thrill in success unless one has been close to failure ... read on.

Yesterday, when I was young, I wanted just two things. One was to grow up and the second was to be a millionaire. I had now achieved one ambition, but have yet to accomplish the other.

It was paper profit, you see; that's all it was. I traded my shares of stock in my twelve corporations for equivalent Saga stock on the Over-the-Counter Market (soon to move to the New York Stock Exchange).

This transaction qualified as a tax-free trade, or pooling of interest, and I was now holding paper worth close to nine million dollars with no more personal debt.

As part of the agreement, I had the right to go to the market with my stock offering and obtain a considerable amount of taxable cash. I timed the offering to coincide with the presidential election of 1972 because I felt Nixon's victory would create a favorable climate for my offering. I had selected my brokerage house (Merrill Lynch) and was ready to go.

I Made a Crucial Mistake

Apparently, Willy the Lock needed some cash and asked me if he could join in my private underwriting and bring in Smith Barney, his brokerage house. They controlled a large block of stock which would almost double the size of my offering. I thought about his request for too brief a period, and then remembering the good deal they had given me, said, "What the hell, go for it!" Was there a mistake in that decision? I'm asking you, what could be the problem?

Think about it, when the market is holding steady why is our offering starting to drop. Can you think of what happened?

Keep thinking.

Keep thinking.

Keep thinking.

Can you believe this? Bad move!

According to my advisors, the market decided this new offering meant the founders were cutting out. The so-called smart money saw the names Laughlin and Anderson and assumed that two of the three Saga founders were dumping a considerable amount of stock. They confused me with Hunk Anderson!

Despite the market moving up with the election result, our stock started a free-fall. Day after day it dropped a little more, from a stock price of $28.5 to $17 in two months, then down to $12. The offering was postponed and finally canceled by me. By the time Willy withdrew his shares, it was too late.

By the way, the overall market continued to move up during this same time period. If you can't run with the big dogs, stay on the porch! I decided to forget about the stock market and go back to work building restaurants.

Chapter 13

The Mystery of Goering & My Yacht

When the debt load fell off my back in my merger with Saga, I felt like a lottery winner. If you win the lottery and live in Seattle, you buy a boat. Seattle is almost totally surrounded by water (Puget Sound and Lakes Washington and Union) and is therefore often proclaimed the boating capital of the world.

I searched for my reward locally first and couldn't find one that suited me, so off I went to Newport Beach, California, another city claiming to be the boating capital of the world. I traveled to the Harbor at Newport Beach to see Big John and his huge converted Navy ship. I arrived too early so I took a side trip with the captain of his boat and we visited the interesting spots along the canals where he showed me a converted Navy ship similar to the Duke's.

I scheduled an appointment for a test run the next day but when I arrived, the captain couldn't get her started. So he asked his mate to take the dinghy and show me the canals of Balboa while he located a mechanic. It was here that we ran across a captivating vision docked in one of the back canals, something called a Dutch botteryacht.

It was love at first sight and I was instantly fascinated. I had the dinghy pilot take me over to her and found the owner who told me a riveting story about how it had been built by Dutch artisans for Hermann Goering.

Goering! My nemesis in WWII!

His air force bombs came too close to my tank a couple of times; thank God they missed.

Making the purchase right then and there, I immediately removed the "For Sale" sign and sent the flustered mate away in his dinghy. The *Groote Beer* was magnificent!

It was odd that even though I didn't get to know Big John better, my meeting with him led me to this amazing find. All oak and hand-carved teak, the boat's unique beauty has created so much interest that I will answer some of the questions frequently asked about her by sharing with you what I know.

Here's the tale; you decide.

Groote Beer translates to Great Bear. She was supposedly conceived circa 1938 in Huisen, 20 kilometers north of Amsterdam, when the boat yard of Jap Kok laid down her 52' keel. She was designed along the lines of the typical "fishing botter" used on the shallow waters of the Zeider Zee (now a lake called the Ijsselmeer) and like all botters, was crafted to be solid and full-bodied, with bluff bows slightly resembling a Dutch clog.

But the *Groote Beer* was head and shoulders above any other botter. Although the construction and shape were traditional, the plan was to engineer a masterpiece of the boat-builder's art that included every possible amenity in an interior laid out by famed designer, H. W. de Voogt.

This was only appropriate, for the owner was Reich Marshall Hermann Goering, Germany's World War I flying ace, national hero and dashing military type.

As Goering's fortunes rose up through the turbulent politics of Germany in the early 1930s, his opinion of himself and his girth expanded, as did his display of military decorations. He had become Hitler's aide de camp and military advisor by the late thirties and was eventually placed in charge of the German air force, or *Luftwaffe,* during World War II.

By the time he commissioned *Groote Beer,* Goering was considered second in command of the thousand-year Reich. As his tastes grew evermore artistic and imperial, J. Kok's botter satisfied his enormous ego's notion of what a latter-day Roman emperor might require in a state barge.

(**NOTE:** There are numerous articles on the Groote Beer but two of my favorite were printed years ago by *Nautical Quarterly* and by Peter Marsh for *Northwest Yachting* magazine.)

As reported by these publications, some believe that Goering took the beautifully carved and gilded botteryacht as his own. The German army was known for confiscating "prized" items from nations they invaded.

The Imperial Field Marshal admired all forms of art. He wasn't a yachtsman but he may have known about the North Sea vessel from Dutch Master paintings.

Goering's plans to use the flat bottomed craft as a show piece with friends and political cronies came to a halt when he was prosecuted by the allies' for war crimes. In 1945, Goering was sentenced to hang by the war crime tribunal in Munich.

A cyanide capsule inside a jar of pomade sealed his fate. Goering killed himself that same night.

To this day, I enjoy the fact that although he had given the Americans a bad time in Germany, I ended up owning the *Groote Beer*. Eerily, Goering's widow died the same year I bought the boat. I looked for a connection but didn't find any.

My Jewish attorney friend delighted in the *Groote* because he had read about another Nazi in the same prison who told this story repeatedly:

Goering was in the exercise yard and when someone mentioned Jewish survivors in Hungary, Goering remarked coldly, "So there are still some there. I thought we had knocked off all of them. Someone slipped up again."

Goering's boat fared better than he did and was completed as he had wished. It was auctioned off by the government in 1948, bought by an import agent from The Hague and eventually owned by Charles Donnelly who had it shipped to Brooklyn. He described the boat as follows:

The planking was oak and the main deck beam consisted of four massive pieces of timber. The entire deck and upper works were teak with a cockpit surrounded with carvings of sea creatures and wonderful gilding everywhere. The main salon even had a fireplace with a Delft-tiled facing.

Her deck was 52.5 feet long, with a wide 18-foot beam, a motor-sailer with a 68-foot mast and over 2,000 square feet of working sail area. She was flat bottomed to stabilize her in rough waters with two solid teak leeboards, one on each side.

Pictures do not do justice to her beauty!

She displaced 38 tons and took over 300 feet to stop once thrown into reverse, which made going through the Seattle locks or docking a real trick.

One owner sailed her in the Transpacific Yacht Race to Hawaii. They came in second to last only because the one boat they managed to beat had lost its mast.

She changed hands a couple more times after that and finally ended up in Newport Beach, California where I discovered her.

I got hold of my sister, Suzanne Peterson, and her husband, John, who were avid boaters and we took my new baby down to San Diego. It made for great restaurant publicity because of its unusual looks and fascinating history.

On our trip up the coast to Seattle, the press coverage continued non-stop. Eventually I moored her at the Seattle Yacht Club where they gave her the number one birth so she could be easily seen by everyone.

Because it had a shallow bottom and no keel, the *Groote* was the only sail boat that could get close to the pier.

It was actually visible from the freeway and drew a lot of attention, exactly what I was looking for. When I had it totally refurbished under the capable hands of Wes Hausman, I discovered that boats are holes in the water you pour money into.

Wherever I sailed that boat, to big cities or smaller ports, media types poured out because they loved the Hermann Goering connection. I once asked a young cocktail waitress in San Diego if she knew who Goering was. She thought for a few seconds and said "That used-car salesman who comes up from Escondido?" Like her, a lot of you people may be too young to know who Goering was, but now you do.

There are those who dispute the history and mystery of the *Groote,* but would she have survived if she hadn't belonged to a Reich Marshall?

The captain's bunk was oversized to accommodate someone of Goering's bulk and it had the large passageways he would have required to maneuver inside. One article I found reported that Goering made 25 trips to the shipyard during the construction phase. Did Goering commission her and did he ever get to sail her? No one knows.

Of course, I choose to believe.

An interior shot of the Groote from a photo used in
The Seattle Times, 10/3/73, in a story about
Stuart Anderson buying the boat and bringing it up north.

This photo ran in *The Port Townsend Leader*, 9/27/73,
in a story about Stuart Anderson buying the Groote Beer
and bringing it up north.

TIP: Any unique thing you
can do is a wise move
because it makes
the restaurant a destination
instead of just a dinner house.

After a time I realized we weren't using the *Groote* enough to justify the money I was pouring into her, so I approached Saga with the suggestion they place it on permanent mounts next to my seafood venture, the *Stuart's at Shilshole* restaurant, which they now owned. They could rent it out for special dinners for four to ten people. A lagoon next to the restaurant made the perfect backdrop. The sheer beauty of her would have enhanced restaurant business but the bean-counter mentality couldn't visualize such a thing, and the answer was a resounding "No!"

Brother-in-law John once asked, "Was it the sailing of that magnificent boat over the beautiful waters of the picturesque Pacific Northwest or was it just for the publicity?" When I don't answer, John says, "Well?"

"Well . . . . I'm thinking!"

I ended up donating the *Groote Beer* to the Sea Scouts, knowing it would be well cared for. I planned to take a tax deduction but never needed to use it because I had a ranch, also known as a money pit.

You've heard the story about the farmer who was asked, "What would you do if you won a million dollars?" He said "I'd just keep farming until it was all gone."

Chapter 14

The Eyes and Ears of the World

Though the small world of Stuart Anderson's Black Angus was driven by the magic big eye of television, I started with the ears of radio in the Seattle market area. Since money was tight, I worked out a trade with local deejays. They could eat and drink on me in exchange for a few on-the-air plugs. It helped me and they had fun swinging with the crowds, a total win-win situation.

The more restaurants we opened, the more sophisticated our marketing became. Haig Cartozian was the genius behind the so-called "Beef Baron," "Steak King," and "Corporate Cowboy" image ... all referring to me, the star. It wasn't done with smoke and mirrors and therein laid the fascination.

Toward the end of the 1800s, James J. Hill planned and built the track of the Great Northern Railway that, centuries later, actually bordered my ranch for miles. He once made this classic statement:

"Most men who have really lived have had, in some shape, their great adventure. This railroad is mine."

Well, the Black Angus Cattle Company Ranch was mine. Purchased by me in 1966, it was comprised of twelve hundred acres and located in Eastern Washington about ten miles west of Ellensburg (the actual address was Thorp).

This was my fourth and last ranch. As time went on I added range acreage by the processes of purchase and lease

Ex-wife Edie and I in 1971: dining with "the girls."

(Quillicine Range) and ended up with twenty-six hundred deeded and twenty-two thousand leased acres.

Finally I could raise cattle while satisfying part of the restaurants' beef needs. However, as the chain grew by leaps and bounds, the scope of the need for beef quickly became too large. And since only twenty-two percent of the animal was used, that left seventy-eight percent of a carcass to get rid of some way or other. I tried trading the unused parts for steaks and roasts but when that became too involved, I reluctantly dropped the practice of furnishing beef. The company then developed very strict specifications and purchased most of its meat from a single supplier.

**I'm at the top, as usual, and Bruce and Ron on the horses.
The caption read** "WHAT'S WRONG WITH THIS PICTURE?"

The message said,
"NOTHING, . . . these three dudes belong on this equipment more
than you think. They also raised the finest quality BLACK ANGUS
cattle in the West. They know their beef . . . and they know how
important it is . . . " **and it went on from there.**

My property evolved into a studio setting for television productions. It was certainly the real thing, including dust, dung, and the sounds of the great outdoors.

Not only did I raise cattle on a grand scale, I had created a stage in the process.

The Yakima River ran through my land as did two major railroads – the Milwaukee and the Great Northern – and it was bordered by Interstate 90.

The potential was there for making TV ads, throwing large private and charitable parties, flying lighter-than-air craft, and raising magnificent black Clydesdales. Since the world has always been fascinated with the Wild West, Haig and I took every advantage of the association.

You may remember the ads that depicted the entire restaurant crew marching through the ranch in their uniforms, carrying plates of sizzling steaks; or the helicopter that landed me and my ranch manager at silos emblazoned with our logo. We then hopped aboard a Jeep and toured scenic areas of the spread. How about the TV skit we did in a chill room at a packing house? I walked by a hanging meat carcass and patted its rump twice to signify it was "choice."

Of course, I got a complaint letter from a TV viewer saying it was a sexist action … and had a little trouble handling the ensuing beef!

Our television presence drew mostly favorable comments and proved to be a powerful medium. More importantly, the commercials were fun and I could do my "outstanding acting" within sight of my house, something not many performers can boast. Andy Warhol says every man has fifteen minutes of fame. I did approximately thirty 30-second commercials. Do the math.

We operated hot-air balloons which created quite a stir along with an entirely unforeseen set of problems. To put it mildly, cattlemen and cattle don't have any great love for those huge monsters.

But it was a thrill to fly over the beautiful Kittitas Valley while a chase car kept an eye on us. There was so much production in the valley, we usually had to float farther than we wanted to in order to avoid crops and livestock.

It was a grand experience when the silence was only disturbed by the occasional firing of gas to keep the balloon aloft. But if you weren't ready for that blast of propane, it shook you out of your reverie and spooked any livestock below you.

Every time we'd pull the cord, the cattle looked up to see where the noise was coming from. When they saw that big thing hanging overhead, all hell broke loose. One cattleman I know even threatened to "shoot the damn stupid thing down."

One incident in particular was
interesting. Some balloons were
flying alongside the freeway and passing
over a herd of livestock … who didn't
even look up.

We finally figured out that these animals
were so used to the noisy freeway, nothing
bothered them.

One of the "fleet" giving rides at a restaurant opening.
It was always nice to have our own bed. We met a lot of
wonderful people in the RV world.

Regrettably, I wasn't even in the balloon basket during our most momentous show because I was attending a football game between the Washington Huskies and the Stanford Cardinals in Palo Alto. At the time, Stanford boasted a fine quarterback with the now-familiar name of John Elway. Boy did he hurt our Huskies bad! That's about all I remember ... and for good reason.

All three of our balloons were supposed to fly over the stadium at half time, an opportunity I thought would make a fantastic promotion. What I didn't know was how close to the stadium's top edge they'd be flying.

As it happened, our seats were near that very same edge and suddenly I heard the familiar sound of propane gas being released. We all jumped about a foot out of our seats as that balloon sailed just a few feet above. If you've never been close to a hot-air balloon you can't appreciate how huge they are and how loud the noise of burning gas is. Within ten minutes, here came the second one – even closer! – and a third closer still. I was more worried about getting arrested than winning the game. Later that evening, at the airport, a man recognized me and came running up and said, "I just have to ask you something. How did you get that one balloon down and back up so fast?"

Come to think of it, who needs a herd of balloons?

The hot-air balloons were a great addition to restaurant openings and special events. We floated them near the freeway during morning drive time on the first day of a restaurant's operation so people would take note.

During the week, we gave tethered rides in the parking lot to reporters, our employees, their kids and customers. The balloons always gave our numbers a shot in the arm in the early weeks at a new location.

As we grew, we keyed our expansion plans to certain TV markets. We felt it took four or more stores to support a strong TV campaign in certain viewing areas and that was usually how we approached advertising in a new city. Of course, this formula also worked well when creating districts for management and supervision.

So, as we moved into Denver, Phoenix, Minneapolis, San Diego, and other locales, we inundated the cities with four or more stores within a period of months.

Does the following ring any bells? "My years as a rancher have given me the edge in selecting only the best cuts of beef for my restaurants," or "… and we'll do the dishes." That was the essence of my TV script for many years. Due to the power of television, wherever I went I was expected to "do the dishes." One of my personal favorites closed with, "You've got my name on it."

Today's marketing has changed considerably with the advent of the internet. In the electronic world – the world of the cloud – you must understand and use every aspect of social media. I don't recommend limiting your database or activity to any one platform like Facebook, because the computer world is moving too fast and it may be gone tomorrow. Use Twitter, LinkedIn and the many others that are out there. Definitely invest in attractive website design and **keep it updated**.

Advertising and the other aspects of marketing are all necessary long-term investments when building both a loyal following and a favorable image in a very competitive business. I'm proud to say that the western-style marketing program, started by Haig Cartozian and me years ago, has been updated by Black Angus' current management.

We are all proud of the excitement our entire package created for customers and employees alike over the years. Haig and I didn't always see eye to eye, but if we'd never disagreed, one of us would have been unnecessary.

A real smart person once said something like this: "Selling without advertising is like winking at a girl in the dark … you know what you're doing but no one else does."

And more importantly, as Confucius says, "If you love what you do, you will never work another day in your life."

From time to time, friends have asked me if I miss the ranch.

I miss the cattle, the dogs and the outdoors, but I especially miss the black Clydessdale horses, those gentle giants that

**The magnificent black Clydesdale hitch:
The Gentle Giants**

added beauty and class to many a parade and store launch. Oversized Clydesdales are somewhat rare even now and when we limited our teams to black, finding great horses with the proper temperament really became difficult.

Most Clydes are brown or bay, such as the Anheuser-Busch eight-horse hitch you've no doubt seen on TV commercials.

Our "boys" from the team also had to be at least seventeen hands high with lots of white feathers on all hooves. It finally became so difficult to locate animals that met our criteria, we had to start our own breeding program. Seeing a new foal was a very special occasion. Talk about becoming attached!

I remember many a parade where those beautiful geldings high-stepped for miles and how the applause encouraged them to step even higher. Hundreds of people lining the route would rise up as we came by and you can guess what they yelled at me: "Where's the beef?"

Stuart with the "boys" from the team.

When we lost a couple of horses along the way, there was real mourning involved. Even now, as I write about those huge horses, I seem to have something in my eye. Yes, parade days have passed and the horses are enjoying their new homes. Time and everything else marches on.

Going once, going twice . . . GONE!

As long as we're on the subject of the ranch, let me tell you about a great auction we held there. A talented cowboy artist by the name of Fred Oldfield knew every cowboy or cowgirl who ever thought of picking up a brush and palette. I knew a ton of cattlemen who also liked art. When we came up with the idea to hold an auction at the ranch in 1980, the "Western Experience Sale" was born.

It was a two-and-a-half day event where we sold highly valued, registered cattle and Western art (some prefer the term "American art") by turns. The animals came from all over the West as did the distinguished artists who brought their very best

Newborn looking for dinner.
They are born light but will turn black.

work. The event included seminars, dancing, "quick draws" (people watching as artists produced something they'd later sell at auction), hot-air balloon rides, and tours of the ranch on a hay wagon pulled by our Clydesdale hitch.

Our finest Black Angus bulls received bids from $10,000 to $100,000 per animal and because of the high buy-in, two, three, or more individuals or ranches would often form a coalition to purchase one outstanding stud bull.

There are two ways to sire quality offspring: breeding a bull naturally on a schedule that alternated between ranches or selling prize semen. A lusty, superior bull will service twenty-five or so registered cows and must be kept in a separate pasture so the parentage of any offspring can be documented through notes and photographs.

I like that word "service."

Around that time, a pill came onto the market allowing a bull to service more than 100 cows instead of the normal twenty-five. I don't know what was in that pill, but it sure tasted bitter!

But back to my story … Have you ever felt like you needed to do something stupid … the urge is there … it's your time? What do you <u>do</u>? You go to an auction … and here I had one built

117

Bless my Mother's heart. She suffered through all my school changes, through my two divorces and much more. I truly could never pay her back but I did take my mother who was in her late eighties to most all the functions and she enjoyed them so much.

right in. Sometimes, you just gotta satisfy that itch.

With me, the itch was scratched by buying cattle, horses, Western art, or farm equipment. I usually went home with stuff I didn't need, had paid too much for and later wished I could take back, a common condition known as buyer's remorse. People like me are easy to spot: we're those overly enthusiastic and frequent bidders the auctioneers are always tickled to see.

This particular evening, Jack Parnell was the auctioneer. He and his crew knew me well and were aware that I sometimes had a devious way of bidding. When a large painting by Joe Bohler came on the block (see photo) that more than resembled an area of my ranch, I fell for it hard.

I didn't bid blind on this one; I had carefully examined the watercolor in advance and knew it would be a good investment. I wrote down my top price and vowed to stick to it – a practice all responsible bidders should adopt – then started in with an amount that was ridiculously low-ball.

With an auctioneer who knew me, such as Jack, I could

HIGH COUNTRY WINTER, Watercolor, 28″x30″

submit a raise without the person next to me even knowing. I could stay in the action invisible and unnoticed. As the price increased, I searched the audience for my competition, feeling sure it was only one person by the way the floor men were acting. But as we were standing in a huge barn and the crowd was big, I had no luck. I was being pushed and – surprise, surprise! – ended up going over my limit.

I bought the painting only to find out that I'd been bidding against my mother! The floor men had never seen her and were therefore unaware of our in-house duel. She was trying to buy the painting for me as a Christmas and birthday present combined. She later said she'd been watching me closely, knowing I had expressed a love for the painting. But since she didn't see me bidding, she kept on going. Not very s-m-a-r-t!

Now I know where that saying, "Quit blaming your mother," comes from.

Of course my poor mother was upset when she found out how much she had helped increase the price but she hadn't done anything wrong. Her kind gesture cost me about a thousand extra, give or take.

So much for secret bidding.

Chapter 15

Split from the Ordinary

It's no surprise that California and Texas have the most restaurants. I recently read in the Nation's Restaurant News that there are over 4,300 restaurants in the Dallas metropolitan area alone. So, once we had California pretty much covered, Texas just had to come next – a great challenge for the Stuart Anderson chain. We had tons of experience under our belt so why not give it a try?

After signing the lease and working closely with city officials on permits, etc., we opened with a lot of pre-publicity. Helen and I went down for the grand opening and, of course, I was in my cowboy hat. When we walked in there were at least 100 other cowboy hats in the room, many with 10X beaver on the inside label. (That's how you can tell quality in a cowboy hat – the X factor.) The men wore expensive western dress and used countrified vocabulary. They also had bigger ranches with more cattle than I, so we didn't exactly knock their socks off. Truth be told, we were lucky they accepted us as well as they did.

It was sticking by our ranching theme that gave us an edge because we had built up a brand that was unique and real. Walking down this path eventually led us into an additional and equally exciting development: In summer, up to 250 of our employees descended on my ranch from all over the country for a three-day meeting, including headquarter executives, restaurant managers and their trainees.

I still don't know of any other chain that does this.

Each management person had to tell us his or her name, what restaurant they were with or what their position was at headquarters. We learned where they were from and where they got their schooling. I was amazed by the clever comments this one or that one made as we moved quickly through the group. And each time he or she heard someone mention the same city or university, they sought each other out and often made a new friend.

Ron Stephenson, my Vice President of Development, was in charge of finding great locations and dealing with all the tough landlords. He gave his name, position, where he was from and when he got to the schooling part, he said he got his education "from abroad." We moved on. It wasn't until a year later, when I got out the old tapes to review them, that I really heard and saw what was going on. Ron appeared to be looking at me and laughing which I hadn't notice earlier in the hustle and bustle.

Now Ron liked to have a good time and had been around the block a time or two so I got to thinking about it. I began to wonder what was so darned funny. When I listened again, I realized that if you separated the "a" and "b" in abroad, you'd get it. I got such a kick out of this whole thing, I told the story at the next meeting and I got all the laughs Ron should have had.

Here's another great story from back in those days: As usual, I was trying to speed up the line to the podium so I called out to one of our managers, "Come on out." I meant to come out of the crowd. But this gentleman, who was gay, hollered back to me, "Stuart, I came out long ago!" It broke the whole place up. This was back in the early 80's when being gay wasn't talked about as much as it is today.

These people had obviously come to have a good time and that we did. We put on skits, played games and generally enjoyed ourselves to the fullest. Of course, it wasn't all play; we did have a variety of legitimate and valuable business sessions.

One example: We gathered up all the groups of restaurant managers and trainees with no management executives allowed. I had each person count by 10s from where they sat or stood, which served to break up their original cliques. After they reassembled, every single person would have a brand new audience with which to discuss the company, including items they wanted to see changed.

Photo by Ken Whitmire

The 1984 managers' meeting at the ranch.

Can you find me?

I used to offer a drink to anyone who could
do that within two minutes.

I'll give you a hint. I'm not in the middle.

Photos by Ken Whitmire

An appointed leader would write down the groups' questions or suggestions and anonymously drop them in a box. After about an hour, I'd clang my famous cowbell and wrangle everyone back to the barn. We then had all of the executives gather on stage. Each person took a slip of paper out of the box, read it out loud and had the appropriate folks answer as best they could. We took some criticism from time to time but I was amazed at how many improvements we made from these suggestions.

That one hour was worth the whole three-day session.

It was such a beautiful sight watching them meet in the pastures, by the creek or in the wooded areas. I enjoyed walking up to our house on a hill above the barn and then looking back down. Picture me beaming with pride at what I had helped to create and the amazing way the ranch worked for this set-up even though it had been designed to raise and feed livestock.

We played hilarious games like donkey baseball where each player was responsible for a donkey and was required to

We held our own Olympics one year.

ride (or drag) that animal to a base or to catch a ball, etc. Need-less to say, those critters were STUBBORN, which helped make this spectacle the silliest thing I ever saw.

One year we had everyone try to catch greased pigs. An-other time, we built a rough, tough golf course with grassy car-pet for greens and organized a tournament. Boy did we lose a lot of balls! We used the pond for rowing races and pressed the vol-leyball and tennis courts into service.

For some reason, the volleyball competition was especially fierce.

At every event, we selected a different group to put on a skit. I remember once when the managers wore tuxedoes on top and shorts on the bottom. When they finished, they bent over and their rears spelled out "Black Angus #1." Of course, each successive year, the new thespians tried to outdo all that had come before – and sometimes they succeeded.

These summer meetings were not only highly productive,

To protect the guilty, no one will be identified.

they allowed our managers to make new friends and acquaintances. We all went back to our jobs with enthusiasm and fresh ideas. Frankly, I seriously doubt that anyone enjoyed these get-togethers as much as I did. And it's just too bad you couldn't have been there with us! You would have loved it.

Chapter 16

Don't Fix What Ain't Broke!

W**e were s-s-s-smokin'!**

From the first twelve Black Angus Restaurants (all originally someone else's, with names like Double Joy, The Polynesian, The Gaslight, The Hideaway, and so forth), we now approached forty-two stores, all "built-to-suit."

This means a landowner would build a restaurant to our specifications and lease it to us. We were moving throughout the West and our future looked as bright as our past. Moving into Canada made us international and we were grossing over one hundred million dollars a year.

It was about this time I realized I had become complacent.

While visiting on the campus with Saga founder, Bill Laughlin, I mentioned that each opening seemed better than the last and used the old slogan, "If it ain't broke, don't fix it!" He came unglued and said, "That's the worst view a progressive businessman can have!" I was surprised at the intensity of his reaction.

I was concerned because, to me, the idea of changing things just for the sake of changing them seemed ridiculous, especially in the restaurant business. I don't mean you shouldn't refine your formula and adapt to changes in the marketplace. But if you're satisfying the customer, stay with it.

**TIP: In this business,
don't anticipate change; stay close to what
your customers and employees want.**

Consult your servers to find out what the customers are saying; they have the closest contact. Ask the dishwasher to report any large amounts of uneaten food he's throwing away, usually a sign it's not making the grade. Allow for customer comments on the back of the sales ticket and read them. Your customer count is your health thermometer. This count should be available every day from your point-of-sale printout, which shows how many meals you sold and what they were. It fluctuates with the weather, new competition, and so forth, but pay attention to it. Compare it to the previous year.

We also calculated, on a weekly basis, the almost one hundred items on the menu according to percentage of sales. Some items would rank fifteen percent, some five and some less than one percent. We usually dropped the bottom item, replacing it with a new one we felt might sell better. That was our extent of "fixing."

I was ready to argue with Bill and then I figured, "What the hell?"

**TIP: Invest in a sophisticated
POS (point-of-sale) system. It can
tell you everything you want
to know and then some.**

Trends are a different subject and they gallop in fast. Early on, when I placed my liquor order for the week, I got a case of gin and one bottle of vodka. I could barely keep up with the switch as it went to a case of vodka and one bottle of gin. In those first years, it was always a shot of whisky and a water or Coke back.

A more dramatic trend is the way lunch habits have changed. Many of us used to enjoy the two-hour martini lunch, which has pretty much gone by the wayside. Maybe that's not all bad but I missed the business. I also was known to participate personally in this institution. What caused the downfall of the leisurely lunch and could we have seen it coming? Yes. The enforcement of drunk-driving laws has greatly affected our serving alcohol to patrons and their consumption of same, a change for the better. Entertainment tax deductions aren't in favor anymore. And think of the recent corporate down-sizing. Employees have to cover more territory now, so lunches have become fast-track meals. You have to identify and stay on top of trends like these or lose good customers.

Then there are established wants and desires we must adapt to. For instance, when we went into the San Francisco area, we discovered that sourdough bread was a must so our ranch bread had to go. In the town of Santa Maria, California, the pressure was on to serve their famous salsa with the beef. We accommodated them. In the city of Tacoma, Washington, we were requested by one group to serve the noon martinis in coffee cups. That wasn't an adaptation, it was just a sneaky ploy caused by a strict employer who would have frowned on a martini at lunch.

These are examples of going with the flow by making small refinements.

What was about to happen to Saga was stunning. This great corporation, which was well conceived and well managed, was about to be turned upside down, with emphasis on down. To this day, I believe its eventual demise was caused by a deep-seated need to **fix it, broken or not.**

Speaking as one risk taker to another (you know who you are) this business can get boring. When things are going too smoothly, there's a tendency to start something new or try to "fix" what we have. A good example was my venture into a new seafood restaurant on the waterfront in Seattle, *Stuart's at Shilshole*. At three stories it was way too big and when people made the connection to me, they expected a great steak.

I ended up selling a lot of meat instead of seafood.

Helen and I lived in a penthouse on the top floor and all I can say is, "Never, NEVER live above a restaurant!"

Shilshole struggled but over time became a success mainly because the waterfront property increased so much in value.

The founders were doing more than a competent job and were certainly not of retirement age, so why did they do what they did – step aside? They ushered in the Charlie and Ernie show starring two new bosses, Ernest C. Arbuckle and Charles A. Lynch. Ernie, a previous chairman at Well's Fargo and former Dean of the Stanford Business School, became the new chairman of our board. He certainly had a strong background, but I don't believe he'd ever seen the inside of a bar.

Next came Charlie (Looking-for-a-Few-Good-Yes-Men) Lynch as Saga's new president. He came from the W. R. Grace Corporation and some other companies before that. Could these two gentlemen, a statistician and a banker, be the guiding lights of a free-wheeling, independent, swinging restaurant business?

But why?

Why indeed!

From the standpoint of the people involved in actual operation of the chain, we had a good working relationship with the founders, the other divisions, and particularly with the Saga personnel with whom we dealt directly. The corporation was strong and the financial community was an indicator of this.

President Charlie was busy at the Menlo Park offices for the first two years and our contact was primarily limited to a hello at meetings. But about the time my company had opened seventy restaurants, Charlie and I had a confrontation over the promotion of my number one gal, "The Iron Butterfly," Bobbi Loughrin, to vice president of administration. I didn't notify Saga of this move until after the fact.

Charlie and Ernie

Charlie became "absolutely infuriated" (to quote him), which got my dander up. I believed his tirade reflected his opposition to my appointing the first female vice president. At all the Saga corporate meetings I'd ever attended, I'd never seen a woman, unlike our managers' meetings. I certainly hadn't needed anyone's hiring or firing approval in my company before but if there was going to be trouble, I wanted to stand on principle.

Chairman Ernie asked if I would drop by his office at the Menlo Park campus. He started in with: "I don't think this conflict between you and Charlie is all that great. The two of you have really just started to relate to each other and you should bide your time on this issue. Give Charlie a little time and the two of you will work well together."

Ernie's conciliatory attitude put me in a mood to cooperate. As my appointment with Charlie loomed, the days dwindled down to a precious few. I discussed the pending confrontation with Bobbi who said, "Please Stuart, don't make me an issue. I don't want it to come to that."

My intuition told me this was a battle I was doomed to lose. I'd been around much longer and was in charge of the fastest-growing and most profitable division in the company, but I had the feeling the founders and the board of directors would back their new president if push came to shove. So I bit my tongue, apologized for not going through channels and let my ego deflate. That's all right; he probably could've fired my ass.

Bobbi kept her title, her raise, and attended the Black Angus executive committee meetings with the other vice presidents. At the first session, without thinking, I asked her to get us coffee but realized immediately what I was doing. She was not a token female. Shame on me! We all got our own coffee, as it should've been.

Another confrontation I had with Charlie concerned a discussion that became somewhat tense when we both started quoting Peter Drucker, the business guru, as if there were two Peters.

Charlie said, "The last thing you do is build your organization around people."

I said, "I perceive the Black Angus chain as one that was built around people."

Without a doubt my greatest asset in the business world was my ability to find individuals with a real talent for the restaurant industry. I had methods that are best described by the saying: "Fit the coat to the man, not the man to the coat."

When you find an outstanding individual, find a position somewhere so he or she can bring value to your group.

For example, one evening, while working late in my office, a young man came in to offer me some advertising in a ski magazine. I had zero interest in placing an ad but I was a ski bum, so I started working with him on trade-outs and swaps. While we chatted, something else was happening: his personality and sincerity appealed to me. When I asked him about his current job he told me it was a dead end.

His name was David Rollo and he eventually became our personnel director. A likeable man with great communication skills, he inspired us all before he died at the age of forty-two.

It was my privilege to give the eulogy at David's memorial service. Let me share with you some of my remembrances so maybe you can know him a little.

If there is a heaven, David's there and I'll bet he's asking a lot of questions. We all smile in our remembering, and that's the way he'd have wanted it.

I liked his style, his manner, his straightforward approach to a new proposal, and he was from Spokane where we were getting ready to open our third restaurant. By the time he left that dark afternoon, I had hired him as an assistant manager at the Spokane store.

David enjoyed telling the story of his first day. For some reason, I'd forgotten to tell the manager, Bruce Attebery, that David was coming. I would love to have witnessed that confrontation!

David Rollo

It was always easy to relate to David because he was never devious. Those who didn't know him well suspected he was naïve but actually, he was simply uncommonly direct and possessed of a trusting nature. His honesty and loyalty were superb and his great laugh was contagious. David, I'm still glad you stopped by that afternoon so many years ago.

This story illustrates just one case of finding an outstanding individual who might come along from any field of endeavor. The vice president of southern operations, Tommy Lee, was a top sergeant in the Army looking for part-time work. He started as a bar-back. Although not a big man, he was big enough to handle two bullies trying to give me a bad time in the bar one night.

Vice President of Development Ron Stephenson started calling on me as a coffee salesman. Haig Cartozian, the vice president of marketing, was a Navy officer who offered to share his table with my foursome at the crowded Seattle Yacht Club after a football game. Bruce Attebery you've already met.

I'm the smartest of all because I always hired people smarter than I.

That Old Gang of Mine
**Left to right: The Black Angus Executive Committee:
Ron Stephenson, Haig Cartozian, Tom Lee,
Bobbi Loughrin and Bruce Attebery**

There wasn't time to discuss all my great hiring abilities with Charlie but I kept pondering these stories as I heard him in the background of my mind assuring me that I had not demonstrated the "complete businessman's competence" in running a hundred million dollar-plus chain. In the next minute, he gave me credit for running the best dinner-house operation in the country. Explain that to me!

Who won? Don't ask me; to this day I don't know. I've heard it said, "If you want to have the last word in an argument, just say okay." Who had the last word? First, last, and always ... Charlie!

If you don't make a plan, you're planning for failure

The plan! The plan! It caused panic every year and at times became an exercise in futility.

Charlie would set the master plan by projecting how many millions it would take to surpass the previous year's results by a healthy fifteen percent, regardless of the reality of the situation. After running it by the board of directors for their automatic stamp of approval, the dollar amounts were split up among the divisions through some formula that no one understood. We, the Black Angus officers, would massage our portion of the plan and resubmit it based on a realistic increase, which was usually somewhat less than the percent Charlie was asking. Then back it would come. I will say that his charts and graphs gave him what he needed to impress the financial community.

We knocked ourselves out because we knew the five-year plan was really a one-year plan and the one-year plan was actually a six-month plan. Now don't get me wrong; planning is an important tool, but the way this one was implemented often seemed like overkill.

To be fair, the plan also had a positive side: it made us study and push our figures around and get to know them like we should. We learned a great deal from the plan even when cussing it and probably spent more time studying it and wrestling with it than on doing the things that would get us where the plan said we should be. Does that make any sense?

And let's not forget those charts and graphs. We didn't call

Charlie "Charts" Lynch without good reason. He was a numbers man, not a people man.

Just when peace reigned over the battleground, here came another biggie. See where you stand on this one.

When do you designate an heir to your throne? Or should I ask, do you ever designate an heir? Charlie wanted me to name the person who would assume my position when I moved on or out. I was reluctant to do so because I had a smooth-working executive committee of four vice presidents, soon to be five. I didn't want to lose any one of them, a definite possibility if they became aware they hadn't been "chosen."

I just didn't want to make that decision to stir up the pot.

There's another factor to consider. (Since I mentioned my greatest asset, it's only fair to mention my biggest liability.) I procrastinate! I wasn't aware of this fact until my cohorts had pointed it out on several occasions. My defensive response was: "It's a method to develop responsibility in others." Bull! I was rationalizing and I knew it. To procrastinate can be a very bad habit. I knew I needed to work on it but I could never decide when.

Again defensively, I'd sometimes say, "Nobody remembers how long it took you to make a decision but how well that decision worked." More bull!

As it turned out, I stood by my decision not to make a decision and I won that one against Charlie because I never did designate an heir.

By the way, Charlie never designated an heir for his position either. This was not significant as it turned out because Saga had only a few more healthy years before it passed into the land of memories.

Chapter 17

Do Unto Others and then Cut Out

Forty years after my stint in WWII, I was once again on the sidelines watching another era draw to a close. As you recall, I thought I'd won the issue with Charlie. Wrong again! And get out your scorecards, ladies and gentlemen – you'll need it to keep track of what Charlie did with my successors.

The person who replaced me in in the job of SAR president was a Saga corporate man selected by Charlie and Jim. Although he didn't have restaurant experience, he was a likeable guy, which made him half right. During his term, company morale began to slip and business began slowing down. Not too surprising that within the year, he was gone.

Next in the parade came a second Saga executive who wasn't given much of a chance but who did quite well in subsequent endeavors.

Not long after, Charlie made still another move in the revolving door of the presidency. (Is everybody keeping up?) As a result of an acquisition of a small group of restaurants, he tapped one of the owners to be in charge of SAR. This third guy went from running a few restaurants to head up a 120-unit chain.

It wasn't that he didn't know; it was more that he knew so much that ain't so.

Our new Mira Mesa restaurant outside San Diego was within a couple of weeks of opening when he came aboard. Guess what? He was trying to **fix what wasn't broken!** He spent over a quarter of a million dollars tearing out booths, replacing them with tables and chairs and remodeling the kitchen to install a rotisserie cooking display. He delayed the opening for more than a month and brought in a new menu.

But hold onto your socks ... you won't believe this one!

Chickens! He had more ways of preparing chicken than Colonel Sanders ever thought of, and more seafood items than Skipper's. Then, to add insult to injury, he added fennel sausages and – wait for it – **rabbit.** Honestly, rabbit was one of the new big feature items!

Thumper didn't belong on a rancher's steak house menu.

From what I heard afterwards, this new president didn't show much respect for the people who built the Black Angus either. As the new menu made its way across the country, the customer count started a free-fall, followed quickly by the profits. What did people go to Stuart Anderson's Black Angus for? A steak, of course. Charlie and this president, with their double egos, felt that steak houses were a dying breed. What a market they missed!

The Outback Steak Houses, our very direct competitor with several outlets in almost every state, started in 1987, one year after Charlie's sale of Saga. Besides Outback, the coming of Logan Roadhouse, Longhorn Steaks, and Lone Star Steakhouse and Saloon created a bull market for steak eateries.

And don't forget Morton's and Ruth's Chris, both in a higher price bracket but still on the move in what should've been **our** market.

When you look at the listing of restaurant chains in the article in Chapter 2's *The Sweet Smell of Success,* not one of these new companies was listed. They were all getting started around the time Black Angus was going to chicken, seafood, and rabbit.

There were three surveys taken on the Stuart Anderson chain just slightly before and during the time frame when all these changes were taking place. The first, which you've already seen, was polled by *USA Today.*

The second was Willy's brain child. He spent a great deal of time (and I understand his own money) to rate the quality of

RESTAURANTS & INSTITUTIONS SECTION 2: CHAIN PROFILES—DINNER HOUSES

CHOICE IN CHAINS
DEC. 19, 1984

THE WINNER AND STILL CHAMP
STUART ANDERSON'S

Single, business-oriented, educated and adventurous are just some of the attributes of the customer who patronizes Stuart Anderson's Black Angus/Cattle Co. restaurants. And once again, those are the attributes of the customer who makes Stuart Anderson's the heavyweight champion of not only the dinner house segment, but the entire full-service segment of *R&I's* Choice in Chains.

The Stuart Anderson's customer, for the most part, is college-educated and earns $25,000 or more a year at a technical, sales, administrative, managerial or professional position. However, the blue-collar worker does not dismiss Stuart Anderson's.

Although more than the average number of Stuart Anderson's customers are divorced, they come to the restaurants in couples. The majority of them fall into two age categories: 50 to 59 and under 30. A good number of their eating-out occasions are business-oriented or are when they try a new eating establishment.

The Stuart Anderson regular usually spends at least $26 a week eating out. The regular's family often spends more than $50 a week. He or she likes to have wine or a cocktail with a meal (the reference to both genders is important because often this cus-

tomer comes from a home with a working woman).

A coffee shop, Mexican, gourmet or Oriental restaurant, quick-service Mexican outlet, deli, steakhouse or ice cream parlor are other favorites of this crowd. More specifically, that list includes Carl's Jr., (another chain heading east across the United States, as Stuart Anderson's is), Straw Hat Pizza, Red Robin, Vie de France, Jack in the Box (another Western chain), Mr. Steak, Sizzler and Shakey's.

A&W, Swensen's, Pizza Time Theatre, Taco Bell, Denny's, Victoria Station, Big Boy, Baskin-Robbins, International House of Pancakes, Arby's and Kentucky Fried Chicken are other chains frequented by this patron group.

Not surprisingly, this patron group tends to order lamb, pork, milk, decaffeinated coffee, eggs, omelets and quiche, Mexican food, regular coffee, healthy foods and salads, and Oriental foods. But trendy foods such as taco salads, croissant sandwiches, guacamole, pasta salads, chicken wings, potato skins, biscuits and sausage, hot-cheese appetizers and specialty burgers also are popular and are ordered often by this group.

Stuart Anderson's Cattle Company Restaurants leads all chains in *R&I's* survey.

140

the food, service, and customer satisfaction, eventually finding them all wanting.

The third survey, also reported back in Chapter 2, was conducted by the respected *Restaurants and Institutions* magazine. They presented an annual "America's Choice in Restaurant Chains Award."

This effort ranked seventy-four chains in conjunction with National Family Opinion, Inc., of Toledo, Ohio. I believe it's a particular honor to receive any award voted on by the general public.

Anyhow ... SAR was voted **Number One** for four of the five years between 1981 and 1985. It was also voted Number One by *USA Today* readers. What I want to ask the Saga founders, especially Willy and Charlie, is:

"What is it about being voted Number One across the country that you want to change?"

Charlie, who seemed overly concerned about showing a rise in quarterly profits, was in trouble and realized his string of successes was coming to an end. Looking back gives you 20/20 vision but it's obvious that the overzealous and unreal shifts made to "maintain company growth" were key contributing factors to the demise of the Saga Corporation. Charlie and the others insisted on running a people business like an organization of bean counters and paid the ultimate price.

With the sagging fortunes of Black Angus and their other restaurants, Saga profits took a dive. Management reacted by purchasing more restaurant companies. In Saga's name, they purchased a Texas chicken chain called Grandy's for 57.5 million dollars ... an amazing price. Two talented entrepreneurs who had done a good job building the chain would do an even better job on the powers that be.

The sale went through without one of us long-time restaurateurs being consulted about any aspect of the transaction. The top five vice presidents of the Black Angus executive committee alone represented more than 105 years of down-and-dirty experience in the trenches of the hospitality sector. Bruce Attebery had designed hundreds of bar and kitchen layouts and knew how to equip same. Ron Stephenson had dealt with over one hundred landlords not to mention the array of problems associated with those locations.

Haig Cartozian knew marketing potential and costs from soup to nuts. Tom Lee knew personnel and morale management. Bobbi Loughrin was more than capable of analyzing the financial reports. And then there was me.

Why wouldn't Saga tap this fountain of information? It wouldn't have cost a dime and could've saved millions.

I was never aware of any action to correct the drop in count or stock value, moves that would have been consistent with Charlie's reputation as a "company turn-around specialist." In very short order, this beautiful company with its manicured campus was shopped around Wall Street. Madness!

Do I sound bitter? Sad is a better word because so few can do so much harm to so many. Have I been harsh? No; these men can take my opinions.

A successful man is one
who can lay a firm foundation with the bricks
that others throw at him.

Sidney Greenberg

Marriott Corporation purchased Saga primarily for the volume-feeding portion of the company and proceeded to sell off everything else including the Black Angus chain. More is coming on that part of my story.

Chapter 18

Boy's, You're Going Down!

A lthough I prefer to share tales that conjure up good feelings, I have to include the following. It hurt and it was more than shocking by the time we realized what had actually happened.

When Marriott bought Saga Corporation, they were only interested in the company's volume feeding deals, preferring to dump all the restaurants. Even with it's revolving-door presidents, the Black Angus Chain had been the cash cow that helped keep some of the other chains afloat.

It goes fast now so hang on and let's keep our spirits up.

When I heard about the sale to Marriott through sources other than Saga Management, I got together with Ron Stephenson (an SAR vice president) and Jack Torre (the contractor who built the new restaurants) to discuss buying the Black Angus Chain. You can see Charlie's response in the letter on the next page, and you may notice that he copied me instead of addressing me directly, never a good sign.

As it happened, the buyers turned out to be two men from W. R. Grace Restaurant Division. (Ooooh, what a coincidence ... Charlie Lynch also came out of Grace. Hmmm.)

Stuart Anderson

CORPORATION

CHARLES A. LYNCH
Chairman of the Board and
Chief Executive Officer

June 3, 1986

Mr. Jack Torre
Torre Construction Company, Inc.
1801 Dove Street, Suite 101
Newport Beach, CA 92660

Dear Jack:

It has been brought to my attention that you are possibly involved with Stuart Anderson and Ron Stephenson in seeking financing to make an offer to purchase Stuart Anderson's Restaurants. Obviously, I do not have this first hand so I merely am making this assumption but felt it important to let you know that if this is true, you should be aware that any discussions are to be directed to and coordinated through:

> Joseph R. Zimmel
> Vice President
> Investment Banking Division
> Goldman Sachs & Co.
> 85 Broad Street
> New York, NY 10004
> 212/902 5536

We have not discussed any such individual divestiture and probably would not be inclined to entertain any at the present time. Nevertheless, Joe Zimmel should be your contact and, obviously, I would appreciate the courtesy of knowing that this is going on.

I might also add that you should consider your involvement in this in light of future business relationships. I certainly would not want any contact with any of the existing personnel in any part of our corporation and, for that reason, I am equally as concerned regarding Stuart Anderson's and Ron Stephenson's involvement.

I pass these comments on for our mutual best interests.

Sincerely,

cc: S. C. Anderson
    R. E. Stephenson
    J. R. Zimmel

ONE SAGA LANE • MENLO PARK, CALIFORNIA 94025 • (415) 854-5150

144

So Anwar Soliman and Ralph Roberts entered the picture and made a very high offer that Marriott couldn't refuse. (See the article below)

From the Los Angeles Times:

Newport Beach Firm Acquires

Restaurant Chains from Marriott

INDUSTRY NOTES
February 05, 1987 | *MARY ANN GALANTE*
Marriott Corp. said it has completed the sale to American Restaurant Group Inc. of Newport Beach of several restaurant chains formerly owned by its Saga subsidiary. Terms of the sale were not disclosed, but sources close to the deal valued it at $280 million.

American Restaurant Group was founded by its largest shareholder, Anwar Soliman, along with several top management executives. To make this deal work, they had to sell the 11 operations in Chicago, an area where we were just getting started and doing great. Chicago always gives me a reason to chuckle whenever I think about one of the openings. I won't name it but let's just say the local officials wanted us to grease their palms … that good old Chicago Machine mentality. We sidestepped the problem by telling them we'd hire their children, wives, nephews and cousins, which we did.

All those jobs are now gone for everyone. Are you ready for this?

One of the very first things the new owners did was pay themselves very high salaries: Anwar made $1,000,000 and Ralph $750,000, plus bonuses. Remember, we're talking mid-1980s when this amounted to serious money.

**Here's some beef for Helen and principals
Anwar Soliman and Ralph Roberts, at a
Henderson, Nevada, opening. I've come
full circle, back to where I began, serving.
I feel the photo of Ralph, who is on the
right, depicts his personality to a tee.**

The huge paychecks at the top didn't help the morale of the other management personnel or our bottom line. In fact, the effect was disastrous.

The next move they made was to get rid of all my experienced and talented management – that old gang of mine, most of whom were axed within the first year. This house cleaning effectively removed me and my influence and my incredible team from operations. Unbelievable!

They raised the menu prices, a stupid move since the company was founded on the concept of great steaks for reasonable prices.

They eliminated TV ads, use of the ranch, the hot air balloons and all the other creative things that had put and kept the name out there over decades of success. They also eliminated all the nighttime entertainment in the lounges so they could "serve more dinners." Does that make sense?

At no time did they ask to see me or consult my opinion on anything. If contacted, I would have suggested they start selling franchises across the East Coast from Maine to Florida. They could have flooded the region with the great name we'd built up over the years, a move I couldn't do during my reign because Saga was only interested in building company owned restaurants.

I knew this counterproductive set of strategies wasn't going to make it because corporate greed will kill even the most successful business.

In January of 1994, *Nation's Restaurant News* reported, "Soliman's American Restaurant Group (ARG) Avoids Junk Default as Leaders Mend." Basically ARG avoided a potential default on its junk bond debt by selling $91.4 million in new bonds and stock. Does this make sense?

In 1997 it was reported that ARG was going to sell its 100-unit Stuart Anderson's Black Angus Chain to a Florida group in order to meet its debt obligation. We all got excited and had hopes that this would bring the chain back to its glory days but our hopes were dashed when ARG cancelled the sale. It was reported that ARG's reason for withdrawing was the financial performance of the Company for the third quarter of 1997.

In 2003 *Nation's Restaurant News* front page read "ARG chief plots split of Angus' 'siblings' to pay debt."

Ralph was installed President and CEO of ARG while Anwar remained an officer of the new company, NBACo (NOT BLACK ANGUS COMPANY) and ARG. A report from 2003 stated that Ralph Roberts had received a base salary of half a million dollars plus $117,000 in bonuses just before filing for bankruptcy in 2004. Bonuses for what? Driving the company into the ground? ARG was supposed to assume the existing debt, which created a lot of unhappy vendors and junk bond holders.

Over time, the company continued to sell off restaurants to pay down the debt and the interest on the debt.

I think around 7,000 jobs were lost. What a shame!

The employees who'd made us successful were well

trained and had worked so hard. Many are still friends today.

Due to the high risk of the notes and bonds, not to mention the outright financial manipulation, bankruptcy was the only solution, not once but twice. In 2009, they were purchased by a management company.

Over the ensuing years, several different management teams have been in control at various times and currently there are 45 surviving Black Angus Steakhouses in six states.

The company recently hired a new man who can boast real restaurant experience. All my good wishes go with him and the company.

Anwar's NBACo doesn't appear to exist any longer.

When Soliman resigned as group executive of W.R. Grace & Co.'s 690-unit restaurant division, he admitted he'd wanted to be as big as McDonald's:

Anwar Soliman's Appetite for Restaurants:
Master Deal Maker Hopes to Build a Company That Will Rival McDonald's

September 20, 1987 | MARY ANN GALANTE |
Los Angeles Times Staff Writer

Oh, please, excuse me ...

Okay, I'm back now ... but they took my name down with them. (Sigh.)

Read on.

Chapter 19

What's in a Name? Your Life!

Have you heard the saying, "A man's good name and reputation is at the heart of his existence?" We spent a lot of time and money putting my name out there what with billboards, TV advertising, newsprint and signs on our buildings, so people knew my name. When my wife makes reservations or appointments, a lot of times they'll ask, "Is this THE Stuart Anderson."

She's always tempted to answer, "No, he's the pretend one."

I remember back when the business was going gangbusters, there came a time when one of the Saga executives asked, almost in passing, if I would give written permission for them to use my name. I was receiving fabulous treatment running a company which I built and loved, so I agreed. It was a small paragraph but a BIG mistake! I wish I had more carefully considered the immense weight of that decision because it allowed the bankruptcy boys to fly my flag over a sinking ship.

Although the headlines blasted *Stuart Anderson's Comes Out of Bankruptcy,* it was not ME. I used to be proud to have my name on the Black Angus Restaurants because it was a successful business and people loved us. After the bankruptcy, I felt like I had a big "B" on my forehead. Some good friends saw the bankruptcy article and jokingly asked if they could send me some money!

Ha-ha.

I was thankful when they changed the name of the restaurants to Black Angus Steakhouse and took my name off the buildings, menus, uniforms, and even my favorite salt and pepper shakers.

Now let me finish with my war stories and a lesson about how important names are.

My War Comes to a Close

We were approaching a temporary bridge at the Mosel River in Germany. The captain in charge of the bridge told me we were the third tank to cross over, a fact that has stuck with me for some unknown reason ...

This was a difficult maneuver because the sheer weight and size of our armored vehicles created visibility problems.

It was bitter cold.

As we got near the other side, I saw some of our troops at a temporary station and a large stack of what I thought was logs. Upon reaching the far bank, I could see that the logs were bodies. It was an unbelievable sight, one I couldn't forget if I tried ... so many bodies stacked so close together, many in their winter German uniforms, but with their shoes off and tags on their toes.

The nearer we got, the leerier I became because I expected the odor would be overwhelming. However, since it was so cold, the bodies were frozen and had little or no odor at all. Once across, we were allowed to pull to the side and let a constant stream of men and machines get ahead of us on the point. What a comforting sight that was.

The farther we traveled, the more German prisoners we saw heading toward us with only an occasional American soldier guarding them with machine guns. Sitting slightly above the eye level of the passing troops, we sometimes exchanged looks. The soldier/prisoners seemed to have no expression. They didn't exhibit hatred toward me and I didn't hate them either. I think we were all wondering why we were there.

During this eerie parade that lasted for hours, no words were spoken. I saw young boys who couldn't have been over 16 and others who looked like seasoned soldiers. They were our enemies, the ones we'd been shooting at and the ones who'd been shooting at us a few days earlier. I even saw one who looked just like my uncle Frank. Boy did that hit home.

I mine some more memories!

All things, good or bad, have to come to an end and my service years were winding down. The early part of winter in Germany was very wet in 1944, either snowing or raining hour after hour with the cold days getting shorter. In fact, that winter set a record for cold temperatures and snowfall. ... ask any man who was there.

The enemy was always close now. In the still of the night we could hear the German tanks moving because, although the power units were very quiet, the tanks' tracks made a squeaking sound. Our Sherman tanks were faster but much noisier and we had a higher silhouette. Also, we mounted 75mm guns while they had those fearsome 88s.

Believe me, we had justification for being more than a little nervous listening to those screechy sounds that never seemed to be either coming or going but just running somewhere off to the side. In exhaustion we eventually fell asleep.

Where and how to sleep each night was always an issue. Usually we pitched a tent but a handy building would suffice if it were close to our armored "home." One night we parked near a dairy barn that had the perfect hay loft to sleep in. There must have been one hundred cows in their stalls for the night. That's one of the world's most pleasant smells to me, wet cow mingled with new-mown hay.

Even more vivid was the subtle noise of all those cows chewing their cud. I can't think of a more satisfying sound. It's like a symphony played by an orchestra of contented animals. Those sounds drowned out the two-part snores- and-fart harmony of my mates and removed the war in a far-off place. I wish I could have said to the farmer, "Bless this barn!" but in Germany during the war, the farms and villages appeared deserted.

151

There were those occasions when we had to sleep inside our tanks, ready for anything. I worked out a system I'm sure other drivers had used before me: I'd wedge my helmet between the gun mount and the side of the tank, then tie the strap under my chin to hold my head up. The next move was to place my booted feet on the still-warm engine mount, close the hatch and drift off to dreamland and a better world.

But whoa...

The feet didn't always stay where they were supposed to and I'd wake up with my boots in an inch of cold water that had leaked through the hatch and soaked clear through to my toes. After a few wet nights and damp, chilly days, I had a hard time walking or even standing when I got out of the tank.

They took me to the front-line aid station where they had to cut my boots off and I saw swollen, blackish feet. Ugly! I was placed on a stretcher and taken to an ambulance with three others who had feet as colorful as mine or worse. We were driven to a field hospital and carried in on stretchers. I told the guys carrying me that I could walk to that tent but one big, tough corporal turned around and growled, "Buddy, if you tried walking on those feet you'd fall on your face."

Now I was scared.

My condition pushed me through the whole medical chain right up to Christmas in an English hospital and my feelings about this turn of events were mixed ... half happiness and half joy.

Of course, my thoughts were with my comrades near the front in that cold weather.

When I was finally discharged a few months later, I had not lost one toe.

My war was at an end.

When I was attending the University of Southern California and got the draft call, I was shocked by my first visit to an induction center. I'll never forget my draft board classification physical in San Pedro, California. I stripped down so different doctors could poke and prod, gauging whether I was fit for service.

The doctor in charge, (of what I' wasn't sure) asked me

how I had acquired the wicked, fixed scar on my hip. When I mumbled "appendicitis" or something like that, which was totally wrong, he gave me a dumb look, shrugged and sent me on down the line. Eventually, I was given my papers classifying me as 1A. Hot dog!

The thrust of this story is that I should've been able to remember and learned how to pronounce a difficult but important medical term.

When you leave the service, the Army gives you an exit physical at no extra charge. When another doctor asked me what the scar on my hip was, I remembered the correct answer: osteomyelitis (bone poisoning). He looked shocked and asked me to repeat it, so I did.

"NO WAY!" he cried. "You must have the name wrong."

I told him, "I'm sure that's the name because I almost died when it came on me as a teenager."

He said, "If that's true, you should never have been in the service. Never!"

I said, "What?"

He said, "You should have been 4F."

It took a spell for this to sink in ... WOW! Being in the service had an impact on my life and I'm thankful I made that mistake. But what might have been ...

Soooo . . . what's in a name, you ask? Well, one name changed my life.

Here's the upshot: not remembering one word, albeit a long and confusing one to a kid, totally altered my whole life. I tell you, I wouldn't trade the high-test excitement, fast pace or unique dangers for anything, not to mention the guys and gals who've disappeared into the mists of time. I'm living the American dream but where I'd be now if I had been ineligible for duty (4-F) is more than I care to ponder at present. Maybe I'll contemplate it tomorrow.

In the grand scheme, I'm glad I screwed up. Otherwise, I might have missed out on a most momentous time of my life.

By the way, that wasn't the first name I'd ever forgotten nor was it the last, as any number of close friends can attest. Dave Rollo, whom you met earlier, had a similar difficulty with names. One day he came into my office excited about a memory improvement class he'd taken. It sounded like a course I badly needed, so I asked him the name of the school. As he struggled to come up with it ... we looked at each other and broke up. I never pursued that class and to this day I'm lousy at names.

Chapter 20

Age is an Attitude

On my major birthday celebrations, I get blasted ... er, I mean roasted, so I send special invitations to my closest friends asking them to take the dais. My 80th was a three-day celebration with the climax being a brunch at Stuart Anderson's Rancho Mirage Restaurant. Here's the save-the-date notice we sent.

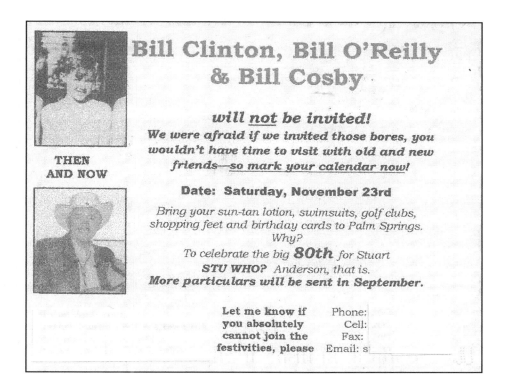

THEN AND NOW

Bill Clinton, Bill O'Reilly & Bill Cosby

will *not* be invited!

We were afraid if we invited those bores, you wouldn't have time to visit with old and new friends—so mark your calendar now!

Date: Saturday, November 23rd

Bring your sun-tan lotion, swimsuits, golf clubs, shopping feet and birthday cards to Palm Springs. Why?

To celebrate the big **80th** for Stuart

STU WHO? *Anderson, that is.*

More particulars will be sent in September.

Let me know if you absolutely cannot join the festivities, please

Phone:
Cell:
Fax:
Email: s

**And here's the cover of the invitation.
Wasn't I the clever one?**

We labeled the name tags according to the different groups we were involved with throughout our life. There was the old Seattle and Whidbey Island friends (Wet Backs - It rains a lot up there, get it?), our motor home friends (Trailer Trash), our ranching friends (Cattle Rustlers), our Desert friends (Desert Rats), relatives (Hangers On), restaurant chain friends (Steak Burners), and Etcetera's (None of the above).

A sample of the silliness follows from one talented old friend whose handle is Pea Dingus. His real name is Bob Case and he's from a cow town named Ellensburg in Eastern Washington. (I'm sure they would rather we characterize it as a college town and it is with an excellent university.)

I sent him the following letter asking him to open the roast and have also included all the correspondence that followed:

Dear Pea Dingus,

Originally I had you teamed with Bob Johnson but he heard you were involved and said he couldn't make it, sooooooo . . . You can do it with your beautiful wife Lovely, or anyone else you might like since you are the star. I can put you with a fun guy from Black Angus days, or you can just do it alone, it's your choice.

You will have a microphone, a spotlight and an old fart's stool to sit on. There will be different teams of two speaking (basically teams from each of the groups.) I will be seated slightly behind the speaker (with a bat).

Joe Mijich, my lawyer and friend, who is great at keeping things rolling, is the talented master of ceremonies. Each team has 3 ½ minutes or less.

A musician will start to play music as soon as you hit the 3 ½ minute mark.

We expect around 300 exciting people from the groups. Although you are not being paid, I expect a sensational performance. Come early.

His response:

Dear Old Man, (He's at least 3 ½ years older than I am!)

First, what in Hell do you mean, I am not getting paid!!!! That better be one hell of a lunch. Are you going to get those 300 people full of joy juice before I get to the mike? There is nothing worse than trying to be funny with 300 old sober bastards ... especially if I am in the same condition.

3 ½ Minutes! It will take me that long to waddle up to the mike. Since I will be all by myself at the mike, I should get 7 minutes . . . and of course get paid double. If you do play music, please don't make it "Blue Suede Shoes" or Old Man will jump up and start performing.

Since there will not be time for any improvising at the mike, I have changed my performance. I WILL WRITE AND RECITE A POEM FOR THE BASTARD, BUT IT MAY TAKE A TAD OVER 3 ½ MINUTES. Your damn music will not stop me from finishing unless, like I said, you play an Elvis song and the Old Man starts his deal.

See you . . . Pea Dingus

From The Old Guy to Pea Dingus:

Dear Pea Dingus,

I'm glad you're coming so I can see Lovely. I'm expecting a fabulous performance. I wanted a picture of you two but understand you want money for that so I called my old buddy Jerry, the Colonel. He will pay me to use this picture of him and his lovely wife, Linda who we call the School Marm. I heard you even tried to get some money from the cashier at the restaurant via telephone. I had warned her and everyone else about you so she refused, of course. Thank you Bob Case for coming all the

Actually Jerry and Linda are a handsome couple and have done very well. He owns property in different California locations and one of them is a "trailer park," albeit a nice one. Not sure what they're called in today's lingo ... mobile home park probably doesn't fly any more either.

way from Ellensburg. Oops, I mean Pea Dingus.

STUART ANDERSON

When I said I'd write a line or two
About this bastard we call Stu
I thought I knew 'bout the life he's had
I knew some was good and some was bad

I said, "I think I'll write about the good"
Helen said "I wish you would"
"But, I don't know how far you'll have to roam
To find enough to write a poem

But if you look back on the life he's had
You just might find enough that's bad
I know enough to fill a book or two
But don't tell him that I've told you

Two things Stu wanted …that's beside his wife
An Armenian Rug and another life
But there was Cartozian … a rug he could bring
A new life was the problem..Stu wanted to sing.

I don't know if you've heard him …. He sounds like a frog
But he can shake and shimmy like wet hound dog.
His idol, of course, was Elvis the King
At every ranch party Stu would get up and sing.

He'd beller and holler it was Elvis at his best.
The crowd would go crazy..Stu'd get no rest.
His legs were aching and his throat was sore.
But his fans kept yelling…More-more-more

As he hammered and stummed on a old beat up guitar
He thought ..If this was the life that made Elvis a star
It looks to me like I've made a mistake.
It's a hell of a lot easier just cooking a steak.

But wait just a minute. I've got ahead of myself
There's a hell of a lot more that's still on the shelf.
That slippery old man can do more than just cook
He sat down and wrote a 300 page book

He handed out books to every one he knew
If you wouldn't buy one he'd give it to you
There is pictures of you in the book…he said
So I bought the damn book and I found that instead

Hell…You were all in the book But I didn't appear
Stu told me later…..I was replaced by a steer.
So much for the book…there's still plenty to tell
About his first business venture….The Caledonia Hotel.

The dollar ninety five steaks were more leather than meat.
So he went up a buck and served steaks you could eat
He said if Wall-Mart can do it with volume and price
I think two ninty five streaks will fit in just nice

That was the start of Stu's Black Angus dream
Bur he couldn't get it done without a great team.
I know that he is happy that you are all here to say
Best Wishes to you Stu on your 80th birthday

There is just one thing that scares the hell out of me
Is there anything more out of Stu that we'll see
You can't have guests for a barbecue
Without using hickory chips from Stu

And when you want to quit and rest your bones.
There's old Stu again with his retirement homes.
Stu…I'm sick of your pictures in a cowboy hat
Standing next to a horse on which you never sat.

Stuart Anderson

The Pea Dingus Poem:

Now, let's move on to my 90th birthday. Sorry to say that a lot of my friends had gone ten toes up so it was a smaller party. I took some excerpts out of the Pea Dingus 90th letter so enjoy.

STU! When you were 80 I wrote you a poem.
My fingers ached right down to the bone.
I think I wrote about the life you led,
But I can't recall...there's fog in my head.
They tell me I said some nice things about you
But my foggy head say's that can't be true.
You thought you were Elvis, I think you recalled
When you got up to sing I sat here and bawled.
I've had ten years to think about the things that I said
And it sounded as though I thought you dead.

It's women like Helen and men like Stu
It's why America prospered and grew.
What the hell, he's only 90 years old.
The kid still has another shot at the gold,
Your Friend, Bob

If you need a smile, I'll give you one of mine.

Final Thoughts, Diabetes Advice and Favorite Recipes

Chapter 21

Inspire Relationships with Payback

It's just impossible not to love the sight of a restaurant full of happy people enjoying dinner, sipping cocktails and appreciating a great crew.

This satisfaction motivated me to get involved with the community ... a kind of payback to those who supported me so much and something I want to encourage you to do before I end my tale.

We should all give back when we can. It takes your time but it helps business as well as your friends and neighbors. Join the local, state and national restaurant associations as well as the Chamber of Commerce, Rotary and other clubs. Volunteer to hold functions at your restaurant. Be involved!

There are many things you can do as a restaurateur: give a percentage of the take on a certain day to a specific charity and advertise the heck out of the fact; hold functions for charity groups at your restaurant, charging only for the actual cost of food and labor if you have to.

These things are payback, a practical way of showing thanks. You can also help by telling others about community events: Put it on Facebook, Twitter, Linkedin, your web site and whatever else is current for your day. Everyone benefits.

As for tending to my own civic duties, I was always ready, willing, and able. If it served some good cause, I was all for it.

american cancer society ● washington division ● march/april 1978

Cancerline

THROW IN WITH THE GOOD GUYS.
FIGHT CANCER IN WASHINGTON.

"Hi, I'm Stuart Anderson. I'm heading up this year's drive for the American Cancer Society here in Washington."

So begins one of the TV spots that will be shown around the state to support the 1978 Crusade.

Stuart Anderson has agreed to be the first Honorary Crusade Chairman in the Washington Division. Anderson is well-known around the state for his Black Angus Restaurants and his Black Angus Cattle Country ranch near Ellensburg, but this is his first involvement with the American Cancer Society. Why did he volunteer?

"I deal with so many people in the course of a day, that while there have been no cancer deaths in my immediate family, I have been touched. A very close friend, who started the business with me, died last year of lung cancer. After a lifetime of smoking 2-3 packs of cigarettes a day myself", Anderson added, "that loss was the impetus for me to quit. It's a ridiculous habit for people to smoke, but sometimes you need a hard blow to come at you like that to do something about it."

As Honorary Crusade Chairman Anderson will be making TV and radio appearances on behalf of the ACS. Volunteers will have to opportunity to meet him at the Crusade Kick-Off meeting in Seattle, April 2.

Anderson was born in Tacoma but grew up in Seattle. After graduating from the University of Washington, he went into the field of hotel management. From there it was just "a skip and jump to the restaurant business." The chain now comprises 41 operating restaurants and 6 others under construction in 10 Western states. Despite growing up in the city, Anderson says he's always had a fascination with outdoor life and ranching ways. He's worked ranches in Quincy, Moses Lake, and Redmond. The ranch just west of Ellensburg has been in operation for 12 years. Although the restuarants do a greater volume of business in other states, he intends to always be headquartered in Washington.

Anderson divides his time between the Ellensburg ranch, his residence at Shilshole, and visiting new restaurants in the west. He has two daughters — Christopher in Bellingham, and Quincy, who is studying art at the University of Washington.

Anderson was last year's Seafair King Neptune Rex, and this year he's chairman of the corporation fund drive of the Washington 4-H Clubs. "You know, until lately I've been so busy I've never been able to contribute community-wise," Anderson says. "I guess you found me at a time when I was more aware of cancer and willing to do something about it. I'm very proud to head-up this year's drive . . . and my goal is to help make it the best ever. Everybody has to help somehow. Everybody has a part of that responsibility."

I was proud to be chairman of the Washington State cancer drive. I worked very hard on it and, as a cancer survivor, I'm glad for all the support they've received.

I was honored to be the King of Seafair in Seattle.
The publicity that went with this was amazing as
we attended parades in a lot of the cities where we
had restaurants such as the Rose Parade in Portland,
the Daffodil Parade and many others.
We usually rode in our specially designed wagon
pulled by our six-up hitch of Clydesdales.

I had the use of a new Corvette
and was escorted to all the functions
with four motorcycle policemen.
I really did feel like a king and may have acted
like one at times.
I'm very thankful Helen hung in there
with me through that ego trip.

Being chosen as the Grand Marshall
of the Ellensburg Rodeo, in Washington State
was special. It is one of the largest rodeos in the
world and draws the top cowboys and cowgirls.
Held over Labor Day weekend, it is well
worth attending.

I was honored to be inducted into the
Ellensurg Rodeo Hall of Fame in 2008.

Grand Marshall Stuart
Stuart was selected by the Ellensburg Rodeo Board of Directors as Grand Marshall of the 1978 Ellensburg Rodeo Parade. The parade was held on September 2 in Ellensburg, Washington.

I got into the speaking game for a few years and was doing pretty well. This one time I stood up to address a luncheon gathering where the conversation was flowing like an ocean and faced an audience consisting mostly of handsomely dressed women. Always nervous before I started a speech, this group was so large and so beautiful, I was even more stressed than usual.

Well, I started in and promptly forgot the next part of the presentation, which happened to be *Hire Smart and Then Keep Them.* I looked at Helen, who was on the podium with me. She immediately understood my predicament and fed me the key words which I picked up on. But then I needed cues again on the next section.

As Helen gave the cues louder and louder, the audience started to laugh. As we got close to the ending and Helen had to be more involved, they laughed harder and harder.

I didn't realize until later they thought it was part of our routine and we were being stand-up comedians. Not true! Of course, I didn't see the humor at first but I persevered and we ended up laughing with them.

This experience spoiled my day and then some. I realized my memory was slipping and my speaking days were over because of my increasing age and the accompanying problems that go with it. That was the last time I spoke publically and I miss it. Hopefully all the previous speaking I did was helpful to many others and their businesses.

Hey, maybe we can become comedians!

Oh, Anderson, Fuggetaboutit.

STUART ANDERSON

Speaker • Author • Restaurateur • Rancher • TV Personality

He did it all and it worked for him!

"HIRE SMART—THEN KEEP THEM." That's one of the business principles that Stuart Anderson, the founder of the Black Angus restaurant chain, lived by as he built his culinary empire. Anderson offers his philosophy to audiences nationwide. His down-to-earth, easy and conversational presentation style captures the hearts and minds of his audience.

Anderson grew Black Angus from a single Seattle bar and café to a chain of 120 restaurants with $260 million in annual sales and 10,000 employees. This is a company that is successfully operating today and was once again voted America's number one choice in the steakhouse category. Stuart illustrates his points with vivid examples and solid techniques designed to advance the bottom line of any business. He's been there and knows what he's talking about.

Photo Walt Mancini, San Gabriel Valley Newspapers

Who else could be more qualified to speak on the following subjects:

- Hire smart—then keep 'em!
- Creative financing
- Marketing—when, how, and why
- Communication—the bridge that binds people to people
- Beef—everything you ever wanted to know but were afraid to ask
- Nutrition and cooking demonstrations

HIS WIFE, HELEN, complements his presentations with her upbeat attitude and sincere interest in helping people help themselves. As a former employee of Black Angus, her perspective on employee retention comes straight from the ranks. Together, Stuart and Helen are able to build a base of solid, proven business principles that you can take to the bank and they have a lot of fun with their audiences while doing it. You get two for the price of one!

When you get involved, you might get lucky
and be on a board with someone like Jane Russell.

She was a co-founder
of (Waif World Adoption International Fund)
which helped find homes for thousands of children.

One other thing I always considered
payback of a sort occurred back in the hay days.
Because we advertised in the football game
programs; because I was a halfback in high school;
and because I loved the sport, I was interviewed
a couple of times before a Saturday game.

Trouble was I had closed down the restaurant the
night before in the wee hours and had to be up,
dressed and perky by 8 a.m.
That was a sacrifice but I guess a way
of giving back.

Last, but definitely not least, is my wife, Helen
who helped me with the book tremendously.
But she also has time to be a board member
for Umbrella Ministries, a support group for mothers
who have lost a child.

If you or someone you know needs help after losing a
child, please check out this website:
www.umbrellaminsitries.org.

Of course, Helen is involved with a number of other
charitable groups. She is an avid and talented beader who
makes and sells awesome jewelry.

Check her out on Twitter @HerasBeadingHaven.

My beautiful wife Helen.

Thank you so much for staying with me!

90 years of FUN... with more to come!

You wanna piece of me?

Well, now you got it all.
On this note, I'm coming to the end of my tales.
I've run out of stories and paper.

I hope you had as much fun reading it
as I did writing it.
It was great having you.

Thank you for staying with me.

Epilogue

....

A Recipe for Good Health

I've been a Type II diabetic since the late seventies. Even so, at age 91, I feel fine, am maintaining a good weight of 174 pounds for my six-foot height and have no major issues. In my hay days, I was 6' 2" and weighed 195 pounds.

My first symptom of this disease they sometimes call "the silent killer" was excessive thirst. When I traveled back and forth between the restaurant and the ranch, I had to drink water the whole way and keep water by my bed at night. When I mentioned this to my doctor, he immediately tested me for diabetes and, sure enough, that was my problem.

I was a little shook up because there wasn't any in my family as far as I knew. I realized I had to learn about this disease and take care of myself. I routinely get an A1c reading from my doctor—my last one was 6.7.

If you don't know your A1c and are diabetic or borderline diabetic, get a new doctor because that's the first thing they should check. It gives a three-month average.

I switched from pills to insulin many years ago at my doctor's suggestion. I poke my finger every single day, twice a day. My daily readings go from 85 to 125 in the mornings and 125 to 200 in the evening before bedtime. I take 23 units of Type N insulin in the evening at bedtime and 4 to 11 units in the morning depending on my reading.

I'm giving you this information because maybe it'll help you compare. I can't stress enough and doctors agree with me that you must continue to test your blood daily.

(**Note:** I'm not trying to play doctor and you should consult yours for the proper program for you.)

I have never tried to hide my diabetes and have been open about it in the hope that I can help others. There are other things I hide but don't bother to ask.

I cannot stress enough how important it is to take care of yourself. Failure to do so can have serious consequences like blindness, organ failure and severe neuropathy. It is estimated that 37 million people are afflicted with diabetes.

I have been promoting eating out throughout this book and you shouldn't let diabetes stop you from doing same. Check the menu on line before you go so you'll know what the healthy choices are. Tell your server you're diabetic and see if they will alter a recipe for you if it is made with sugar. Asian foods can be high in sugar but you can order a good stir fry and just use low sodium soy. Ask them not to bring the dessert menu.

Forget about "dieting," you have to learn different ways of eating. By cutting out white carbohydrates like white rice, white bread and white pastas, you are three quarters of the way there. There are great whole grain alternatives; Helen often uses almond flour instead of regular flour and the results are delicious.

The glycemic index (GI) measures how long it takes your body to process food. For example, different types of potatoes have different glycemic index levels with the gold potatoes being the best.

One easy way to identify healthy food choices is to look for the **GI** symbol. Eating properly should help you feel fuller for a longer time, in turn controlling appetite. I won't get into the details on this but you can go on line and get an Glycemic Index for everything you eat.

And since we all indulge way too much, let's talk about sugar. Studies show that eating sweets causes you to feel hungry sooner so it's important to look at carbohydrates when you buy anything. Even if the label reads "no sugar added" or "sugar free," a carb is still a carb and when broken down through digestion, is reduced to a simple sugar.

You couldn't guess how many food items contain sugar – even things you'd least suspect, like catsup. Happily, there is a reduced-sugar catsup with one sugar carb per serving. And did you know that a cup of non-fat milk contains 12 grams of sugar? You might try substituting almond or soy milk. Amazingly, once you delete sugar from your diet, your sugar cravings will go away.

Chocolate is an example of a food that can be good for you but be sure to choose dark or bittersweet chocolate or one that has at least 70% cocoa. Helen makes great "cookies" from a recipe on the Fiber One cereal box that satisfy the sweet tooth I was born with.

You just melt 12 oz. of dark chocolate chips (she uses about a third sugar free chocolate chips and two thirds dark chocolate chips) and half a cup of peanut butter and mix it with one package of Fiber One cereal. This simple treat will provide a tasty and satisfying dessert minus the guilt trip.

One brief mention of fats: Once we discovered how most oils are processed, we decided to stick to cold pressed Extra Virgin Olive Oil or Coconut Oil with some good old butter once in a while. Other cooking oils, including Canola Oil, come from modified grains and use solvents to extend their shelf life making them truly toxic. Check this out on the Internet.

If you are looking to improve your eating habits and sugar intake in a big way, you might want to check out *The Abascal Way* by Kathy Abascal or *The Blood Sugar Solution* by Dr. Mark Hyman. Both have delicious recipes.

BLACK ANGUS FAVORITES AND HELEN'S EASY FARE

Let's start off with some Stuart Anderson's Black Angus favorites from the old days: the "scalloped" potatoes, the garlic and cheese breads and bleu cheese dressing.

BLACK ANGUS POTATOES AU GRATIN

This was a much-requested recipe in the early days when this was the only alternative to a baked potato served at a Black Angus Restaurant. *Gratin* means dishes cooked with grated cheese.

Serves 4 to 6
1 ½ lb. potatoes
Salt
2 T. (1/4 stick) butter
1 T. finely chopped onion
1 garlic clove, minced
2 T. flour
1 1/2 cup hot milk
1/2 cup shredded sharp cheddar cheese
1 tsp. freshly grated Parmesan cheese
Salt & freshly ground pepper or seasoned pepper
1/2 cup shredded cheddar
2 T. grated Parmesan
1/2 tsp. paprika for topping

Boil unpeeled potatoes in lightly salted water until tender. Cool, then peel and cut into 1/4" slices. Layer slices in buttered casserole.

Preheat oven to 350 degrees. Melt butter in medium saucepan, Sauté onion and garlic until translucent and stir in flour until mixture is smooth. Gradually add hot milk, stirring constantly. Stir in 1/2 cup cheddar cheese, 1 teaspoon Parmesan cheese, and continue cooking until cheese is melted. Season to taste with salt and pepper. Pour over potatoes in casserole, sprinkle with cheeses and paprika, and bake for 25 to 35 minutes, or until golden brown.

POTATOES DAUPHINES

Helen prefers this recipe from *Bon Appétit Country Cooking* but it is very rich and should be a rare splurge. She uses Yukon Gold potatoes.

> *2 cups milk*
> *6 T butter*
> *Salt and pepper*
> *2 lb. potatoes*
> *1 clove garlic, crushed*
> *2 cup cream*
> *Nutmeg (optional)*
> *½ cup grated Gruyere cheese*

Boil the milk in a large heavy pan. Add the butter and season with salt and pepper. Meanwhile peel and wipe the potatoes with a clean cloth (do not wash them). Then cut them into wafer-thin slices. Put them in the boiling milk and add the crushed garlic. Simmer very gently until tender and the mixture thickens a bit.

Add the cream, simmer for a moment, check the seasoning and grate in a little nutmeg if desired.

Transfer to a buttered earthenware gratin dish and sprinkle with the grated cheese. Cook in a moderate oven (350F) for 15 minutes, until the top is well browned. Serve hot.

ORIGINAL BLACK ANGUS RANCH BREAD

*1 loaf French bread or combined French
and sour dough
1 cup bread crumbs
1 cup Parmesan cheese
2 T. garlic powder
2 T Serves 8
Dash paprika
1/2 cup (1 cube) butter*

Mix crumbs, cheese, garlic powder, and paprika thoroughly. Melt butter. Dip each slice of bread into the butter, then into the topping. Bake at 450 degrees four to five minutes. I prefer a toaster oven. And now you know!

BLACK ANGUS GARLIC/CHEESE BREAD

*1 loaf French bread Paprika
Garlic/cheese spread as follows:
1/4 cup (1/2 cube) butter or margarine
2 large cloves garlic
1 1/2 tsp. lemon juice
4 oz. each jack & cheddar cheese, shredded
2 T. grated Parmesan cheese
1 T. mayonnaise
1 T. minced parsley
1/4 tsp. oregano, crushed dried leaves*

Make garlic spread by combining butter, lemon juice, and garlic and mix well. Combine mixture with mayonnaise, parsley, and oregano and blend. Add cheeses and mix again. Split loaf in half horizontally. Spread each half with the cheese/garlic mixture. Sprinkle with paprika. Bake at 350 degrees for 5 minutes and then place about 6" under the broiler for another 3 to 5 minutes until it's golden brown (watch carefully so it doesn't bum). Cut and serve in napkin-lined basket.

BLEU CHEESE DRESSING

This is one of the easiest dressings to make and much tastier than anything you can buy in a jar.

1/3 cup mayonnaise
1/3 cup buttermilk
1 tablespoon lemon juice
1/8 teaspoon cracked black pepper
1 pinch salt
1/2 cup blue cheese, crumbled

Mix first five ingredients well. Stir in bleu cheese. Refrigerate at least 1/2 hour before serving.

STUART & SARAH'S BEAN MIX

Those of you who have enjoyed one of the great meals in the big party barn at the ranch will no doubt remember the wonderful baked beans. Well, now you can enjoy them in your own home. Of course, simmering in that pot over an open fire stoked with special woods for flavor probably had something to do with the beans' unique taste.

Serves 20
1/2 lb. thick-sliced bacon, diced
3 medium onions, diced
1 1/2 cup ketchup
2 1/2 tsp. BBQ spice (a dry spice
available at grocery stores)
3/4 cup brown sugar
3 cans (28 ounce each) B&M baked beans, drained

Sauté the bacon until half cooked. Add onions and sauté until translucent. Add remaining ingredients and simmer uncovered for 1/2 hour. Drain the beans and add to mixture. Simmer for at least 1/2 hour.

Note: This bean mix can be made and frozen before the beans are added. You can then use it as needed for smaller quantities.

ERICA SALAD

We stopped at a beautiful Black Angus cattle ranch at the foot of the Sierras in Gardnerville, Nevada, where we were greeted by Jim and June Rolph. We struck up one of those instant friendships while we caught fresh trout out of their pond and ended up staying for a wonderful dinner and fun evening. Jim did a lot to keep the Black Angus breed pure. June served this salad that night.

Serves 4 to 6

6 T. vegetable or olive oil
3 T. vinegar
Salt and pepper to taste
1 sweet onion, chopped
1 pkg. frozen or 1 can drained,
French style green beans

4 hardboiled eggs, chopped
3 T. mayonnaise
1 tsp. prepared mustard
2 tsp. vinegar
1/2 tsp salt.
4 strips bacon
1 head lettuce, new leaf, butter,
or other curly-leafed type

Combine oil, vinegar, salt, pepper, onion and green beans in a bowl. Combine eggs, mayonnaise, mustard, vinegar and salt in another bowl. Fry bacon until crisp. Crumble into small bits.

To assemble, put beans on a bed of lettuce, put egg mixture on top, and finish with a sprinkling of bacon crumbs. Delicious.

SPICY COCKTAIL NUTS

This is a great snack – very healthy – and it has a little pizzazz. It's designed to break apart in chunks, kind of like with peanut brittle and makes a nice hostess gift in a cute bag or box. From *Giada's Feel Good Food:*

1 large egg white
1 C roasted & salted almonds
1 C hazelnuts, toasted (see directions below)
1 C walnut halves, toasted (directions below)
¼ C sugar
1 T. Madras curry powder (I used regular curry)
1 ½ tsp. ground cumin
1 ¼ tsp. garlic salt
½ tsp cayenne pepper (less if you don't like it hot)
½ tsp. ground cardamom
¼ tsp. ground cinnamon

Position rack in the center of the oven and preheat to 250 degrees. Oil a baking sheet liberally with olive oil or spray.

In a large bowl, whisk the egg white until frothy. Add the nuts and stir until coated.

In a small bowl combine the rest of the ingredients and sprinkle this mixture over the nuts and toss until well coated. Arrange the nuts in a single layer on the prepared baking sheet. Bake until golden and fragrant, about 45 minutes. Set aside to cool for at least an hour.

Using a metal spatula, remove the nuts from the baking sheet. Break the nuts into bite-sized pieces and put in serving bowls or store in plastic bag after cooling.

To toast: Bake hazelnuts in a 350-degree oven on a baking sheet for 8-10 minutes and let cool before using. Do the same for the walnuts except 6-8 minutes.

BREAKFAST STIR FRY

Many morning meals in our kitchen consist of a mostly egg white stir fry. For a diabetic, protein is a great way to start your day. Experiment with this recipe to suit your taste. Sometimes we use leftover salmon instead of sausage or whatever works. When using salmon, add a little dried dill weed as a seasoning.

Serves 2
1 chicken sausage (We use feta & spinach sausage)
2 large mushrooms, halved & sliced
1 kale leaf (use scissors to cut into thin strips)
(Greens are optional and you can use spinach
if you prefer)
Coconut or virgin olive oil (we like the coconut flavor)
1 egg
Liquid egg white (about ½ C or more if wanted)
Trader Joe's 21 Season Salute if desired (no salt)
Salt & pepper to taste
Cheese of your choice
(Adding sautéed onions or garlic is tasty too)

Put oil in heated fry pan, add sausage and mushrooms and stir until they start to brown, stir and add kale and continue stirring until kale or spinach wilts. Add egg, egg whites and seasonings and stir with spatula until cooked. Remove from heat and grate cheese on top.

P.S.
Many say liquid coconut oil is really good for the memory. Buy the pure expeller pressed oil that says MCT's (medium chain triglycerides). Start off with ¼ to ½ tsp. daily and gradually increase because too much too soon can make you run to the bathroom.

Again, check this out on the internet and consult with your doctor.

BREAKFAST BISCUIT BRULEE

This was a Pillsbury Bake-Off recipe by a Gail Singer and another Stuart favorite. There are whole wheat refrigerated canned biscuits if you look for them. This is an easy recipe to half if you buy the smaller container of biscuits. This is a treat and not served often at our house because of the white carbs.

Serves 8
2 eggs
¼ C heavy whipping cream (have used half & half)
1/8 tsp ground nutmeg
2 (6-oz.) containers 99% Fat Free French Vanilla Yogurt (We use lite with less sugar)
1 (16 oz.) can Pillsbury Grands, flaky layers refrigerated original biscuits
1/3 C sugar
3 T butter, melted

Heat oven to 375 degrees. Spray 8 (6 oz) ramekins or custard cups with cooking spray or rub with butter; place on baking sheet with sides.

In medium bowl, beat eggs, cream, nutmeg and yogurt with electric mixer or wire whip until well blended.

Separate dough into 8 biscuits; separate each evenly into 2 layers, making 16 dough rounds. Place sugar in shallow dish. Brush one side with butter and press in sugar. Place one dough round in bottom of each ramekin.

Spoon ¼ yogurt mixture over dough round in each ramekin. Top with remaining dough rounds after you have buttered and sugared them.

Bake at 375 for 20-26 minutes or until tops are deep golden brown. Cool 15 minutes before serving.

BAKED STEAK WITH MUSTARD SAUCE

This recipe comes from our good friend, Cyndy. Throw some new red potatoes in the pan, dribble a little butter on them, season, and let them cook alongside the meat.

Serves 4
2 ½" sirloin steak, 2 lbs.
Salt and freshly ground pepper to taste
1 medium onion, finely chopped
1 cup catsup
3 T. butter, melted
1 T. lemon juice
1 small green pepper, sliced
Fresh chopped parsley, 1 small bunch
Worcestershire sauce, a few drops

Preheat broiler. Place steak 4 inches below broiler. Sear both sides. Remove from oven and drain off fat. Season with salt and pepper. Mix all ingredients and pour over steak in pan. Place in 425-degree oven for 30 minutes. Remove from oven and transfer to a platter. Pour mustard sauce over, sprinkle parsley on top and serve.

Mustard Sauce:
2 T. butter
2 T. barbecue sauce (any commercial brand)
2 T. Worcestershire sauce
2 T. dry mustard
2 T. cream
Mix all ingredients with melted butter, except cream. Heat over a medium burner until bubbly. Add cream and heat just until hot but don't boil. Pour over baked steak and serve.

BRAISED OXTAIL WITH CELERY HEARTS

We've enjoyed this dish many times. It is delicious with oxtails or beef short ribs and using both works great in case someone is squeamish about oxtails. My mother used to call them ox joints because she thought it sounded better. This recipe came from *Time Life Books' Foods of the World.*

3 lbs. oxtail
Salt and pepper
Flour
3 T olive oil
****

2 C finely chopped onions
1 Tsp. finely chopped garlic
½ C dry red wine
1 C beef stock
1 ½ C Italian plum or whole pack tomatoes,
Drained and coarsely chopped
1 T tomato paste
4 Whole cloves
****

2 C water
1 celery heart cut into 2x1/4" julienne strips

Preheat oven to 325. Season oxtails with salt and pepper, then roll the pieces in flour (or shake in a plastic bag with the flour). Brush off excess and brown the pieces in a heavy skillet on high heat with the olive oil. Brown all sides, 5 or 6 at a time, turning with tongs and then transfer them to a heavy 3- to 4-quart flameproof casserole. Discard excess fat from the skillet, leaving only a thin film on the bottom.

Add the finely chopped onions and garlic and cook them over moderate heat, stirring frequently, for 8 to 10 minutes, or until they are soft and lightly colored. Pour in the red wine and boil it briskly over high heat, stirring constantly. When the wine has cooked almost completely away, stir in the beef stock, cook for a minute or two, then pour the entire contents over the oxtail. Add the drained tomatoes, tomato paste and cloves.

Bring the casserole to a boil over high heat, cover it and place in the middle shelf of the oven, regulating the heat if necessary to keep the casserole at a slow simmer.

Meanwhile, cook the celery strips in the 2 cups of boiling water for 5 minutes. Drain and set aside. When the oxtail has cooked for 3 ½ hours, gently stir in the blanched celery. Cover the casserole again and cook for another 30 minutes. Skim off as much fat as possible from the sauce and serve the oxtail directly from the casserole.

MARINATED FLANK STEAK

Fire up the grill for this one. It's delicious.

Serves 6
1 1/2 lb. flank steak 3/4 cup oil
1/4 cup soy sauce 1/4 cup honey
2 T. vinegar
3 T. onion, finely chopped
1 large clove garlic, minced
1/2 tsp. ground ginger

Score flank steak on both sides in a diamond pattern and place meat in a shallow pan or a large plastic baggy. Combine the rest of the ingredients and pour over the steak. Marinate in the refrigerator all day, or overnight, turning occasionally.

Broil 5 to 7 minutes per side, depending on how you want it cooked. Slice very thin across the grain to serve.

SWEDISH MEATBALLS

These are always popular with our guests and we love them. They are lighter than most meatballs.

¾ lb. ground beef
½ lb. pork sausage
¼ lb. ground veal
½ C minced onion
¾ C dry bread crumbs
(Helen substitutes gluten free
bread crumbs mixed with almond flour)
1 T snipped parsley
2 tsp. salt
1/8 tsp pepper
1 tsp. Worcestershire sauce
1 egg
½ C milk
****

¼ C olive oil
½ C flour
1 tsp. paprika
½ tsp. salt
1/8 tsp. pepper
2 C water
¾ C sour cream

Mix thoroughly onion, crumbs, parsley, salt, pepper, the Worcestershire sauce, egg and milk and then add the beef, pork, and veal. Get your clean hands in there and mix well. Refrigerate for a couple of hours or overnight.

In large skillet, heat the oil, roll meatballs into the desired size and brown, turning so they're brown all the way around. Remove meatballs and keep warm.

Blend flour, paprika, ½ tsp. salt and pepper into oil in skillet. Cook over low heat, stirring constantly until mixture is smooth and bubbly. Turn up stove to medium heat and gradually stir in water using a wire whisk. Boil and stir until thickened and smooth. Reduce heat and gradually stir in sour cream, mix until smooth. Add meatballs and heat thoroughly.

SKILLET CHICKEN ROASTED POTATOES & CHICKEN

This was in a magazine and was from Jerry Seinfeld's wife Jessica's, *Can't Cook Book*. This is really easy and very good.

Serves 4

      1 yellow onion, thinly sliced
      ½ cup water
      5 medium Yukon Gold potatoes (about 1 ¼ lbs.)
      sliced into ¼" thick rounds (We use less.)
      1 T extra-virgin or regular olive oil
      2 T fresh rosemary leaves (2 sprigs)
      I use less as I don't like a strong rosemary taste
      1 ½ tsp. kosher salt, divided
      ¾ tsp. black pepper, divided
      1 T ground coriander
      4 bone-in, skin-on chicken thighs and
      4 bone-in, skin-on chicken drumsticks

Heat the oven with the oven rack in the low position to 425 degrees. Scatter onions over the bottom of a large, ovenproof skillet. Add water. Lay the potatoes over the onions. Drizzle with the olive oil. Sprinkle rosemary leaves over the potatoes, along with 1 tsp. salt and ¼ tsp. pepper.

Combine the coriander with remaining salt and pepper. Rub pieces. Lay chicken, skin side up over the potatoes. Roast until chicken is cooked through and potatoes are tender—about 1 hour.

CRISPY PORK CHOPS

This is one of my all-time favorites. The trick is to have the pan hot enough at the start so they brown quickly.

*Trader Joe's 21 Seasoning (we use this in many
things; it adds great flavor)
Salt and pepper (love Crescent Seasoned Pepper)
Pork chops (bone in and thin cut)
½ C water, more if needed*

Season the chops and then brown in hot olive oil on both sides. Add a little water, about ½ cup, quickly cover, turn temperature way down and simmer for 45 minutes to an hour. Check periodically so they don't get dry. Add water as needed. If there is a little coffee left from earlier in the day, you can put a little of that in when you first add your water.

We add gold or red potatoes sliced about 1½" wide the last half hour. Baste them with some of the liquid and add a little salt, then let them simmer. Bottom side will be nice and brown.

Serve with no sugar added apple sauce and a good vegetable and you have a healthy and easy dinner.

Stuart Anderson